I0796281

Foreword by Beth Moore

The only thing I love more than talking about books is reading one. Little gets me more worked up than hearing from publishing friends what projects they're excited to release. During one such conversation, a good friend of mine at Tyndale House mentioned a concept in the conversational phase among their staff about a kids' storybook Bible depicting the magnificent diversity of God's colorful family. The hope was to capture a child's imagination with the vivid and very real gospel of Christ.

I was delighted.

"If you were doing the choosing," he said, "who would you pick to write it?" That would be the easiest question I'd get all week.

"Esau McCaulley!"

I was so convinced of it that, even when they circled back around a few weeks later, unsure if he would take on the immense project with so many other things on his plate, I didn't budge.

"It's Esau!"

Mind you, none of this was up to me and, if this hadn't been a fun conversation between friends and publishing colleagues, I wouldn't have been so bold. I could hardly have been more pleased when I soon heard Esau had accepted the project.

I'd like to tell you why.

I'd met Esau a year or two earlier by way of a Zoom interview. We come from different worlds within Christianity, so it wasn't a given that I'd find him so accessible and fascinating. Sometimes we who are not academics imagine that many who are academics can't speak our language or share our same passions.

I knew twenty minutes into the conversation this was a man with no small enthusiasm about the Bible and matters of faith and community. The die was cast for an unexpected camaraderie that I will always cherish.

Still, I was taken aback poring over the pages of *Reading While Black*. I anticipate being able to say to my last breath that it was among the best books I've ever read by a living author. Though the podcast conversation and the book were enough to make me want to read everything Esau would ever publish, I'm not sure they would have been enough for me to think this storybook Bible would flourish most in his capable and creative hands.

Actually, Esau's love of children and his desire to see their faces in a book did it. Forgive my slant, but I have a hard time not being partial to a person who appears to live within his home what he teaches from a lectern. Simply put, he's not only a theologian, he's a family man who loves his wife and is crazy about his kids. Regarding the latter, I don't mean from a distance. He served his wife, US Navy Captain Mandy McCaulley, by keeping their home well afloat while she was on duty serving our country. Perhaps you can tell I'm as much a fan of Mandy's as I am Esau's.

These factors alongside his beautifully written children's books made him, in my estimation, the perfect writer of this storybook Bible. But, goodness knows, I can be wrong. So, man, was I ever glad to hold the manuscript in my hands and see that, at least on this one occasion, this girl was on target. With great joy and a heart teeming with enthusiasm, I invite you into the pages of *God's Colorful Kingdom Storybook Bible: The Story of God's Big Diverse Family*, masterfully written by Esau McCaulley and gorgeously illustrated by Rogério Coelho.

If I could drop a storybook on the doorstep of every household with a child inside, this would be the one.

Theologically sound and visually beautiful. Combining McCaulley's sharp scholarship and storytelling with Coelho's delightful and often breathtaking illustrations makes for a children's Bible worth sharing with all the little people in your life!

PHIL VISCHER, filmmaker, creator of *VeggieTales* and *What's in the Bible?*

Tyndale House Publishers
Carol Stream, Illinois

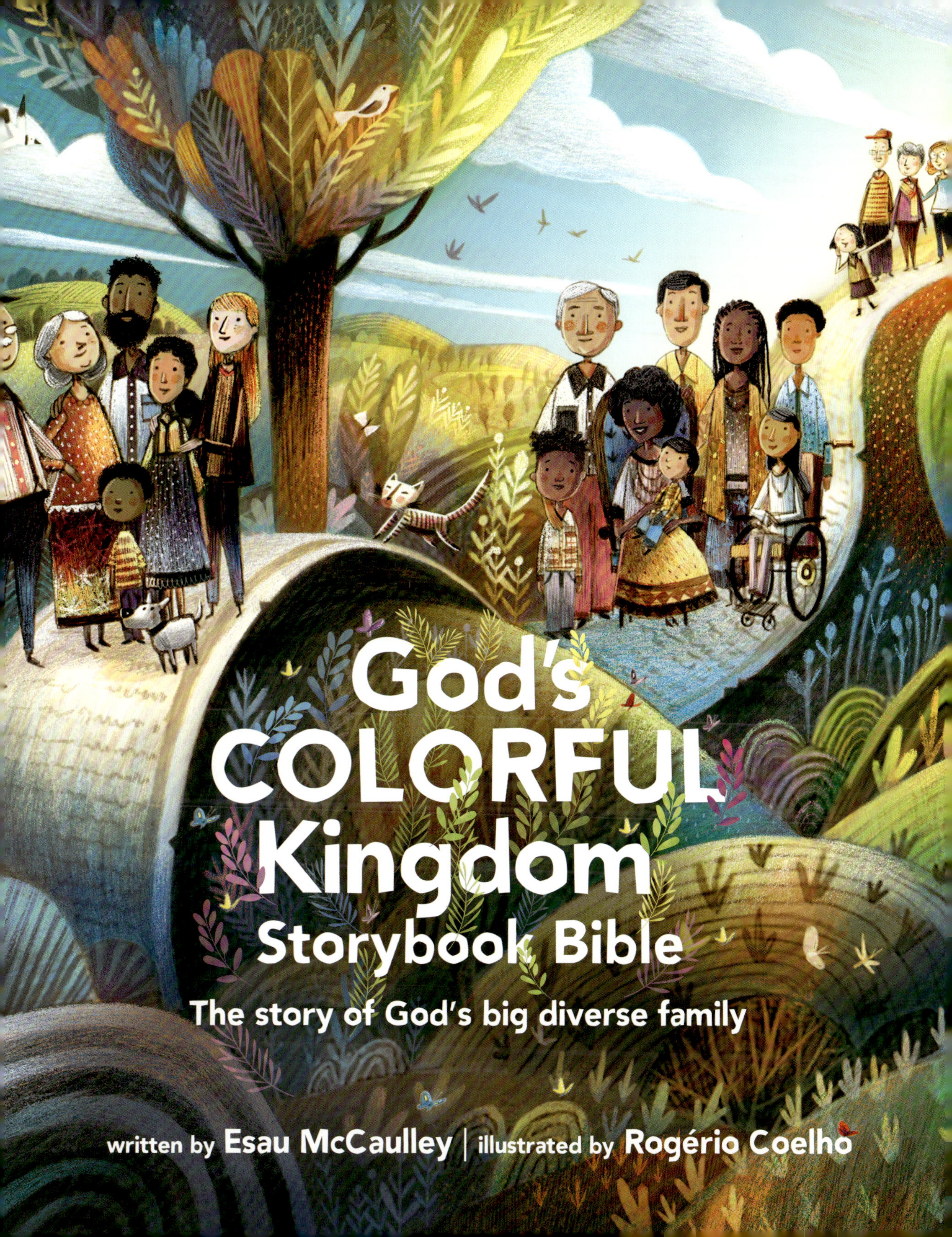
God's COLORFUL Kingdom
Storybook Bible
The story of God's big diverse family
written by Esau McCaulley | illustrated by Rogério Coelho

Visit Tyndale's website for kids at tyndale.com/kids.

Visit the author's website at esaumccaulley.com.

God's Colorful Kingdom Storybook Bible: The Story of God's Big Diverse Family

Spot illustrations colorized by Olivia Jensen

Designed by Jacqueline L. Nuñez

For manufacturing information regarding this product, please call 1-855-277-9400.

For information about special discounts for bulk purchases, please contact Tyndale House Publishers at csresponse@tyndale.com, or call 1-855-277-9400.

Library of Congress Cataloging-in-Publication Data
A catalog record for this book is available from the Library of Congress.

ISBN 978-1-4964-5988-6

Printed in China

31 30 29 28 27 26 25
7 6 5 4 3 2 1

This book is dedicated to my four children
(especially our two youngest, Peter and Miriam).
May you always find hope and joy in God's Word.
It is a gift to us for our good.

Contents

A Note to Parents, Caregivers, and Teachers

I would like to tell you a story—but not the whole of it. Who could tell the complete story of God? Not even the Bible can contain the entire narrative of what God does in the world. That's because the story of the world from beginning to end is God's story. He's in every nook and cranny—whatever nooks and crannies are—of every tale. This book, dear reader, is an attempt to tell thirty-one stories from Scripture that highlight two central themes that occur over and over in the Bible itself.

First, I want to tell about God's love for the many nations—or ethnic groups—of the world. God makes it clear on just about every page of Scripture that his desire is to form a very diverse family. The unity in diversity of the church is a testimony to the universal power of the gospel to draw people to the living God.

Why tell this story now? We live in a world that likes to divide people up based on how much money they make, the color of their skin, or where they are from. The stories in this book will show children that God's family is not like that.

We also live in a world where many people are sick, poor, needy, and hurting. Does the Bible say anything about how we as Christians should think about these people? Indeed, the Bible has plenty to say, and stories about justice for the marginalized will be highlighted in this book as well.

I am attempting to emphasize these stories while staying focused on God as the Hero of the whole story and on the great salvation that Jesus brings us. I'm drawing attention to these two themes in the Bible while hopefully never getting off track from the grand narrative that the Scriptures declare about God and his gracious love for us.

If you and your children read these stories the way they are intended, you will not leave these retellings with more things to do, but with a greater appreciation of what God has done and a greater desire to join in the work that he has never stopped doing.

This book is the beginning of an adventure with the Scriptures themselves, and I hope it leads children to a lifelong love of God's Word.

As the narrator, I will be jumping in and out of the story explaining bits and trying to bring key ideas home to children. My intention, even when I paraphrase passages of Scripture, is to tell the story as faithfully as I know how. Consider this book an invitation to a much bigger story that still fills me with wonder.

Esau+

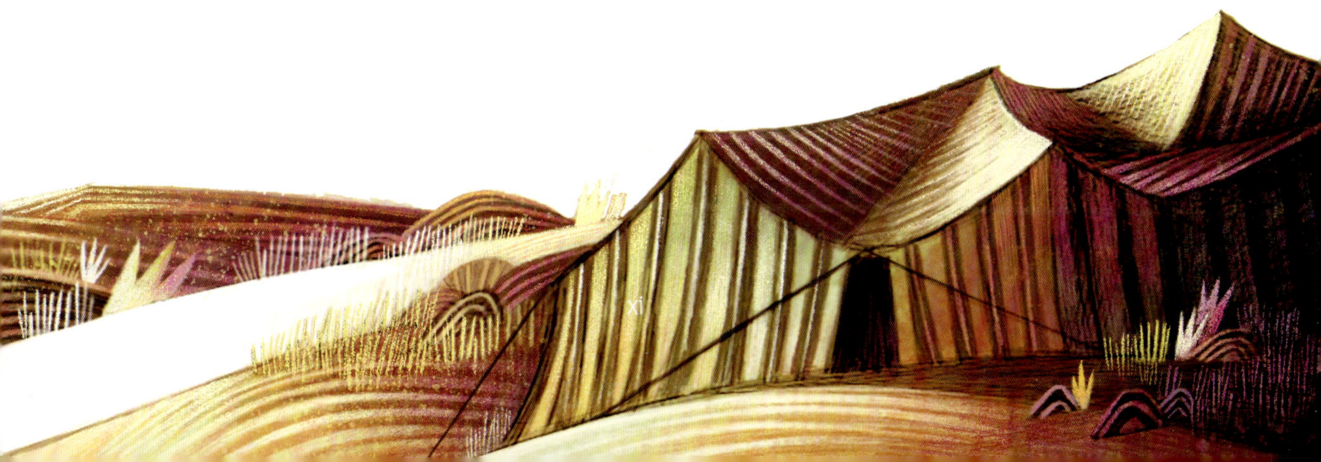

GENESIS 1:1–2:3

Creation

In the beginning God created the heavens and the earth.
Genesis 1:1

The story of the Bible does not begin with you and me. It starts with God. If we can imagine it, God existed before there was a before. He has always been here.

One writer says it this way: "Before the mountains were born or you made the earth, from everlasting to everlasting you are God" (Psalm 90:2). Just thinking about that gives me a headache. It also makes me want to sing songs of praise to God.

God is the superhero. He is the star of everything that happens. We are here, the world is here, the stars, the animals, and the plants are here because "in the beginning God created the heavens and the earth." He wanted it to be, and so it is.

This is good news. No one is a mistake. God created us for a reason. He likes what he has made. We know because he told us.

God looked at the stars he made as they lit up the sky,

and he called them GOOD.

God looked at the fish he made as they swam in the blue sea,

and he called them GOOD.

God looked at the animals he made as they roamed the earth with their hooves, horns, snouts, and claws,

and he called them GOOD.

God looked at the sun he made as it gave light to the day and the moon he made as it welcomed the night,

and he called them GOOD.

God enjoys when created things do what he made them to do.

The plants he created to grow on the earth glorify God by GROWING.

The animals he created to wander the land glorify God by WANDERING.

The birds he created to fly in the sky glorify God by FLYING.

And you, dear READER, by being the boy or girl God created you to be, glorify him by just being. Much of this is very simple. You glorify God by eating, growing, and attending school and church. You glorify God by being kind to your brothers and sisters and listening to your parents.

If God gave you a love of singing, you can glorify God using your voice.

If God gave you a love of sports, you can glorify God through athletics.

If God made you a dancer, you can glorify God by dancing. You can write, sing, play, or draw to the glory of God. One day you might even glorify God by being a doctor, chef, firefighter, pastor, or teacher.

When God made the world, he didn't make it all green or all blue. He didn't make all the snowflakes the same shape. He didn't make only dogs or only rabbits. No. God made a diverse world containing every imaginable shape and color. He did this because he loves diversity.

God saved his best, most creative work for last: Adam and Eve.

He made the first humans in his own image. Humans are unique because we can say thank you to God for all the good things he made.

God gave Adam and Eve the command to be fruitful and multiply, which means he wanted them to have children!

This command led to the creation of new families. God loves to fill the world with people made in his image. Men and women come together as husband and wife to make more image bearers. This has happened over and over since the beginning of time. It is the reason why you and I exist.

All of us are made in the image of God. It doesn't matter if you were born into a rich family or a poor one—you bear God's image. You are valuable to God.

We all look different from each other. Our skin may be dark or light. Our hair may be curly or straight. We come in many shapes and sizes. It doesn't matter. God still looks at us and calls us good.

The belief that God made us all in his image gives strength to

people whom society treats unfairly. It encourages Christ followers to fight for fair treatment and a chance to live and work without being harmed. It inspired African American Christians to fight against laws that denied their rights for many years. They knew that God had looked upon them and called them good.

The most wonderful thing that the world has ever seen is God's own Son, Jesus. He existed with God the Father before there was a star in the sky or a fish in the sea. He is the true image of God. He showed us through his life what God is like. He set the story right when things went wrong. But we are getting ahead of ourselves. More on him later.

GENESIS 2:4–3:24

The Fall: Things Go Wrong

The man and his wife heard the sound of the Lord God as he was walking in the garden in the cool of the day, and they hid from the Lord God among the trees of the garden. But the Lord God called to the man, "Where are you?"

Genesis 3:8-9

God had made the world and all its beautiful diversity. It had flowing rivers and flopping fish. It had dazzling evenings as the sun dipped below the ocean, allowing the sand upon the beaches to become a theater where you could lie back and watch each star make its debut. But there was no one to write poems and songs about beaches and stars. There was no one to draw pictures of animals and mountains. There was no one who could say thank you to God for all the beauty he had made. But God wasn't done creating. He saved his best for last.

God's most glorious creation was the humans Adam and Eve, our first parents. Humans were such a good idea he told them to make more of themselves. God told them to become a huge family.

God put Adam and Eve in a garden. He gave them the important job of tending to and caring for it. Having work to do is one of the things that makes us feel alive. Learning, reading, playing, and cleaning in the good world God made is part of why we are here.

Work is good for us. We were made to work and live.

God gave Adam a command he was supposed to share with his wife, Eve. Adam and Eve could enjoy the good place that God made for them. They could eat any food except the food from one tree: the tree of the knowledge of good and evil.

Every story has a bad guy, and this one's no exception. The bad guy in this story is the serpent, Satan—the stealer of joy.

The crafty serpent came to Eve and Adam with a question: "Did God really say you can't eat from any of the trees of the Garden?"

The serpent was trying to make God look selfish or cruel. But God isn't stingy with his gifts. Sometimes he tells us no to keep us safe. Like when a friend yells *Stop!* just before you fall into a muddy puddle.

Eve knew that God was not stingy. She told the serpent, "God has given us *food from all the trees except one*. If we eat from that tree or even touch it, we will die." (God didn't make the no-touch rule. Maybe Adam and Eve decided to add that bit just to be safe.)

The serpent lied. He said, "You won't die. God doesn't want the best for you. He wants to keep *you* from becoming like *him*, knowing good and evil." This is the same lie the evil one tells us today—that God doesn't know what is best.

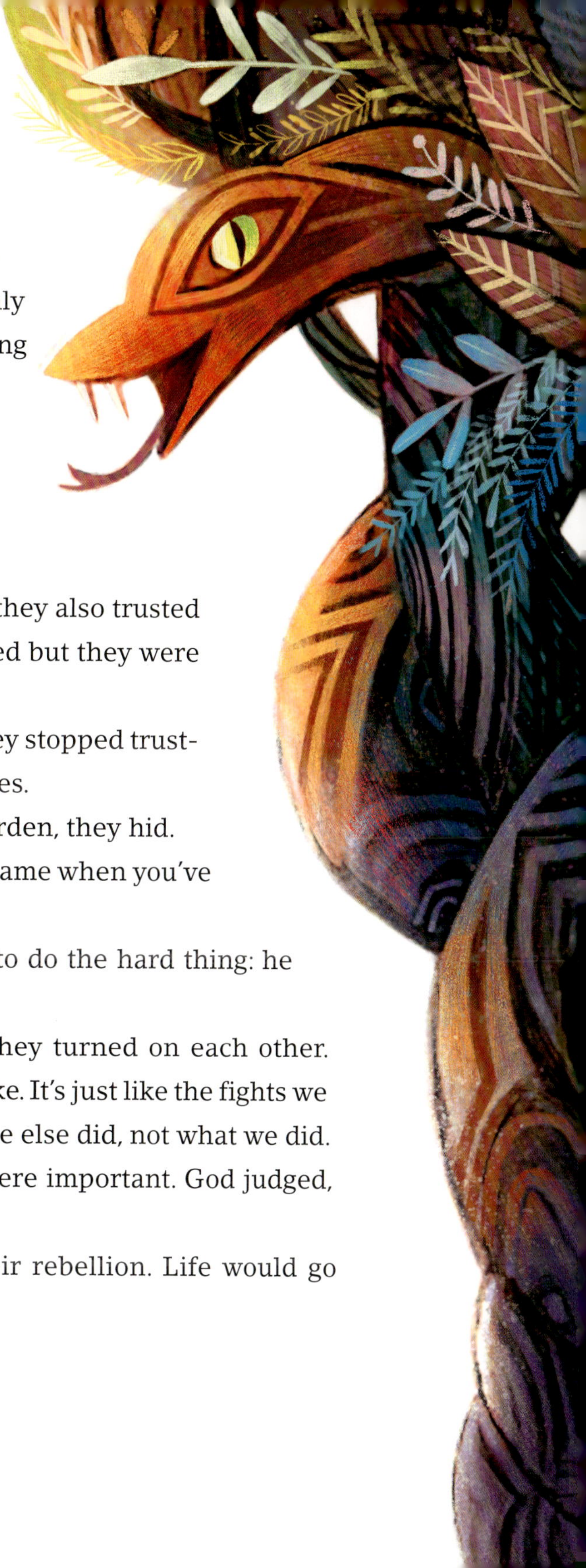

Satan's lie was a very strange one because God had already made Eve and Adam in his image. They could only become more like God through obeying his commands, not through disobeying.

But Eve and Adam believed the lie. The food from the tree looked tempting. They ate.

Things went bad from there.

When Adam and Eve obeyed God, they also trusted each other completely. They were naked but they were not embarrassed.

Once they stopped trusting God, they stopped trusting each other. They covered themselves.

When God came to them in the Garden, they hid.

This is shame. Have you ever felt shame when you've done something wrong? I have.

God loved Adam and Eve enough to do the hard thing: he made them face what they had done.

It may come as no surprise that they turned on each other. Adam blamed Eve. Eve blamed the snake. It's just like the fights we have at home. We look at what everyone else did, not what we did.

Two things happened next. Both were important. God judged, and God showed mercy.

God judged Adam and Eve for their rebellion. Life would go

forward, but it would be harder. Pain and sin and death were now in the world.

Sin is rebelling; it is rejecting God's good plan for us because we think we know better. When we sin by lying, for example, it's because we believe that dishonesty is better for us than the truth God calls us to tell.

Sin is in every person in the whole world. It affects all of us in different ways. Sin causes some people to be cruel, to be unkind to people who don't look like them. It causes some to be greedy and not want to share all the things God has given them.

Sin causes problems, but sin is not all-powerful. It does not have the last word because it did not create the world—God did. He never stops caring for us. With God's help, we can resist sin. We can be better. We can begin again.

After Adam and Eve disobeyed, life went on. God made a promise that someday one of Eve's descendants would have a child who would defeat the enemies of humanity: sin and death. Jesus was part of God's plans even before things went wrong. He has always been a light in dark places, pointing us forward.

GENESIS 6–10

The Water and the List

The sons of Ham: Cush, Egypt, Put and Canaan.
Genesis 10:6

The people God formed were creative. They made cities and art and music. They sang, they danced, and they made clothes, shoes, and tools. Cities and villages sprang up that were as diverse as the people God made. Careers were born. There were storytellers, healers, warriors, farmers, and shepherds. People discovered new ways to make food, and different flavors clashed together for the first time. (I'm pretty sure pizza wasn't invented yet—that took a while.)

Storytellers passed down wisdom, and parents taught their children to talk and walk and live. Mom and Dad showed little girls and boys how to garden, hunt, and build things.

But humans also sinned. We sinned a lot. We hurt each other; we killed. We robbed the poor and were cruel to the weak. We treated life like a game where you did everything you could to win, even if that meant breaking the rules or even breaking other people. We worshiped false gods. Sin's impact continued to grow. Sin spread like a virus. It seemed like everyone was sick.

God did not like the sickness of sin. He did not like the way humans treated each other. God decided to send a flood to punish the world for its rebellion. But he also showed mercy. He told a man named Noah to build a large boat and bring all the different types of animals on board. Noah's family and the animals would be safe on the boat.

Noah must have been shocked when God told him to build that huge boat! He must have been shocked that God spoke to him at all. And then there was the problem of his friends and family. What would they think of a huge boat built so far from the water? What would they think of Noah wandering around the area, chasing squirrels and lizards for a boat trip?

Noah probably wondered, *Why does God care so much about the animals anyway? Would he really miss geese?*

Then Noah remembered that God was planning to rescue the animals and Noah's family because God is gracious. He loves all the wonderful creatures that he has made. Even when God judges, he finds room for mercy. This is good news.

The Flood came and much was destroyed, but the people and animals on the boat survived.

After the Flood, God made a promise. He said, "I will never again judge the world by a flood." God's promise to show mercy gave Noah and his family hope in a dark time.

After Noah's family left the boat, God gave them the same command he gave to Adam and Eve: "Have lots of children. Fill the world with people who bear my image."

The Bible gives us a list of these people who began to fill the world. At first, the list might seem very boring.

I will give you a sample from Genesis 10:13-14: "Egypt was the father of the Ludites, Anamites, Lehabites, Naphtuhites, Pathrusites, Kasluhites (from whom the Philistines came) and Caphtorites."

That was about as exciting as reading a sheet of math problems. Why does God put all these names after the story of the Flood? The names represent different ethnic groups, nations, and communities. They form a list of all the people who came from Noah's three sons.

And this list isn't just a bunch of names. This list tells a story. When you say the names of your parents and grandparents, you aren't just saying names. Those names carry the story of you with them.

Names represent lives of joy and pain. You are the result of those stories, even the difficult ones. You are good news. It does not matter how you came to be here—you are a gift. You are a story.

This list of names from Genesis is really just part of a longer list of *our* family members. They tell the story of how we came to be. These names are a reminder that no matter where you are from or what color you are, you are an important part of the human family created by God.

God doesn't rank humans or make one bunch better than the other. No one group or nation can claim to be better than another, because we are all family. But God gave us this list of names for an even more important reason than that. The whole human family, even after the Flood, still needed rescuing from sin. The problem of sin wasn't fixed yet.

In a few pages, we are going to meet a man named Abram. We'll see God give Abram a mission to bless the world. Who makes up this world that God is sending him to bless? The nations and ethnic groups on the list!

God's plan has always included rescuing people from all the nations of the world. God has always wanted a large and diverse family, and we're about to see that plan unfold.

GENESIS 11:1-9

Babel: Coming Together for the Wrong Things

Now the whole world had one language.
Genesis 11:1

Sometimes you get together with your friends or family to do things that are good and fun. Maybe you go to the beach and decide to build a sandcastle. Or you might gather with your siblings to play a game of Monopoly or make some homemade pizza.

Other times, people get together to do something bad like be mean to the new kid at school. Groups can be tricky. This is the story of a tricky group.

After the Flood, God told the people to multiply and fill the earth with people who reflect his image. But they came up with a different plan.

The people started to move east to a place called Shinar. But instead of continuing to spread out and form new communities, they decided to stop. Maybe they found a good spot next to a body of water, or maybe the grass grew a little higher in that area. Maybe

the sheep and cattle were just tired. Maybe the people were tired. Road trips exhaust me, and I'm in a car, not on foot or on the back of a donkey!

Stopping is easy. Moving forward can be hard.

Instead of filling God's wonderfully diverse world with more people made in God's image, the people decided to build a city and a tower. They got together and decided, "We're good at making bricks. Let's make some bricks and mortar and build ourselves a city. Let's make homes for our families and a market to trade our crops and meat. Let's build our own independent life that no one can take from us. Our city will be known all over the world! We'll be famous!"

God doesn't hate cities or bricks or towers. The problem was that this city had a bad purpose. The people wanted to build it to make a name for themselves.

What does it mean to make a name for yourself? It means to do something that will be remembered. These people wanted to be the stars of the story. They did not want to use their creativity to glorify God, but themselves. Becoming famous can make us believe that we don't need God or other people. Things always go wrong when we make ourselves the heroes in God's story.

Humans are good at lots of things, but God is the best at taking care of us. When we depend on ourselves instead of him, trouble is around the corner.

The people in this story also wanted to avoid being spread all over the earth. The world can be a scary place, especially at night. Sometimes it seems safest to hide where you feel comfortable. But God promised to be with his people wherever they went. Refusing to move was refusing to trust that God had something good in store.

The people were able to work on this tower and this city because they all spoke the same language. One person could say, "Pass me the brick," and the person next to him would understand what he meant.

The people were very impressed with their city and tower. Their freshly made bricks looked perfect in the moonlight. But God was not impressed. From the perspective of the God who made the world, the city and tower were like a preschooler's scribbles in the dirt.

God loves the things we make if we make them for the right reasons, but this tower was made for the wrong reasons. It was an example of people getting together for bad instead of good.

God stopped their work by causing the people to speak different languages from one another. Now when someone said, "Pass me the brick," his neighbor no longer understood. They couldn't keep building the city if they couldn't talk to each other. Instead of letting the people keep working together to do evil, God separated them so that they could spread out and do good in the world. Sometimes being told no is good for us, especially if it stops us from harming ourselves or others.

It might be easy to think a variety of languages was the punishment in this story. That would be wrong. God always wanted his people to spread out and create new things. God's judgment was also an act of kindness.

The human family was never meant to be divided forever, though. God had a plan to bring his people back together again. This plan began with one person. A guy named Abram. We'll meet him soon.

GENESIS 11:24–17:27

God, Abraham, and the Very Big Promise

All peoples on earth will be blessed through you.
Genesis 12:3

Sometimes the Bible can feel like a very big story. And it is! It is the story of a very big God who created everything we see, touch, and feel.

At other times, the story of the Bible can feel very small. The whole scene fits inside a bedroom or a closet.

In the story of Abram, God's story shrinks all the way down to a talk between God and one person. Small stories can have very big consequences. (*Consequence* is a fancy word for "result.") This small story had consequences big enough to change the world.

The story started with Abram's father, Terah. Terah decided that he wanted to make some changes. He left his home of Ur and traveled to a place called Canaan. But Terah never made it to Canaan. Instead he chose to settle in Harran. Terah died in Harran, and his son Abram continued to live there.

All that changed when Abram had the most unexpected encounter of his entire life: Abram met God! God told Abram to leave his family and home. How could Abram explain this change of plans to his wife and relatives? "We are moving because the God who made everything came to me and told me to get going"?

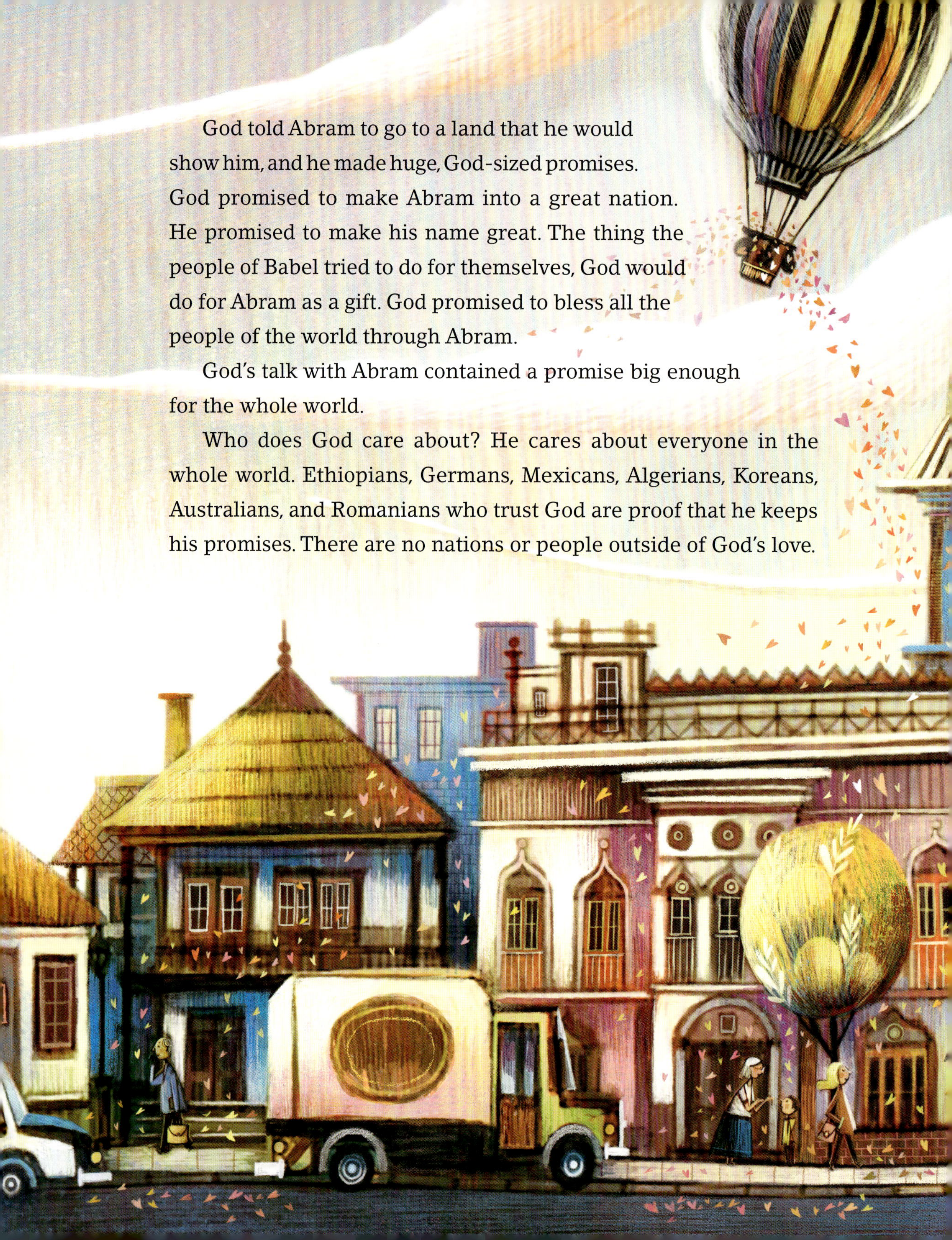

God told Abram to go to a land that he would show him, and he made huge, God-sized promises. God promised to make Abram into a great nation. He promised to make his name great. The thing the people of Babel tried to do for themselves, God would do for Abram as a gift. God promised to bless all the people of the world through Abram.

God's talk with Abram contained a promise big enough for the whole world.

Who does God care about? He cares about everyone in the whole world. Ethiopians, Germans, Mexicans, Algerians, Koreans, Australians, and Romanians who trust God are proof that he keeps his promises. There are no nations or people outside of God's love.

God did not choose Abram because he was special. Abram was special because God chose him. God's promises must have seemed impossible to Abram. His wife, Sarai, had been unable to have children. The idea of Abram's family becoming a large nation probably seemed as likely to him as waking up with the ability to fly or turn invisible.

The hardest part of any promise is waiting. God promised a lot to Abram, but his life remained difficult. It was dangerous. Abram was already an old man, so he probably feared that he might die too soon to have any children of his own.

One night God took Abram outside and told him to look up. Sometimes God has to do that. He has to take us to a place where we can see what is possible with him.

God told Abram to count the stars if he could. Have you ever tried to count all the stars? It can't be done! God said, "The number of the stars is how many descendants you will have." Abram believed what God promised, and his trust pleased God.

God warned Abram that things would be hard. "Your descendants will be slaves in Egypt for four hundred years. You will die of old age and rest in peace. After their slavery, I will bring them into the land that I promised you."

God made a covenant with Abram. A covenant is a deal between two people. Normally both sides have to promise something. For example, if you agree to clean your room in exchange for ice cream, there are two sides to the agreement. You have to clean, and your parents have to supply the ice cream.

But in this covenant, only God had to do something. Abram didn't have to do anything just yet. This is good news. If it had been up to Abram, he might have found a way to mess it up. But since it was up to God, the promise was sure to happen. All of Abram's hopes were based on how trustworthy God is—and so are all of *our* hopes.

God kept his promise. Abram and Sarai had a child named Isaac even after they were very old and it seemed impossible.

God gave Abram and Sarai new names. Sarai's name was changed to Sarah, and Abram's was changed to Abraham. Abram means "father," but Abraham means "father of many." The "many" are all the different types of people who would come from Abraham and his family. You can't even say the name of one of the most important characters in the Bible without hearing about God's love of diversity. God blessed Abraham, the father of many nations.

GENESIS 18–48

Joseph and His Two Sons: Ephraim and Manasseh

Now then, your two sons born to you in Egypt before I came to you here will be reckoned as mine; Ephraim and Manasseh will be mine.
Genesis 48:5

God kept his word: Isaac was Abraham's promised son. It would be through Isaac and his children that God would do great things for the nations.

Isaac had two sons, Esau and Jacob. God chose Jacob to continue his plan to bless the people of the world.

Jacob had a lot of children: twelve boys and one girl. Joseph, one of the boys, dreamed about some interesting things. With great excitement, he told his brothers and parents about these dreams. He said, "I dreamed that you all bowed down to me! All of you, including Mom and Dad."

Anyone who has a sibling can understand why Joseph's dreams did not go over very well. His brothers thought, *Who does Joseph think he is, our king or something? We'll show him how we feel about him and his dreams.*

Joseph's brothers decided to do something very cruel. One day they caught him far from home. They jumped him, stripped him of his robe, and threw him into a pit. Joseph was terrified and devastated, betrayed by those who claimed to love him.

His brothers sold him into slavery, and eventually he was taken to Egypt as a slave. He even went to prison after being accused of something he didn't do.

While Joseph was in prison, he met Pharaoh's cupbearer. Pharaoh was the ruler of Egypt, and the cupbearer's job was to make sure Pharaoh's food was safe to eat.

The cupbearer had gotten into trouble with Pharaoh and was put in prison. He worried that he would never work for the king again, and he had a dream about his future that he asked Joseph to explain.

God helped Joseph understand what the dream meant. "You will

get your old job back," Joseph said, "and when you do, remember me." Pharaoh did hire the cupbearer again, but he forgot about Joseph.

One day Pharaoh had a dream that needed interpreting. The cupbearer finally told Pharaoh that Joseph could make sense of dreams, and Joseph was released from prison.

Joseph told Pharaoh his dream was about a famine that was coming soon. (A famine is when a country doesn't have enough food to feed its people. I don't mean not enough food for second helpings at dinner. I mean not enough food to live. When this happens, people often leave the place where there is no food and go to a place that has food. This was true in Bible times, and it is also true today. Many people in the world lack enough food to eat.)

Pharaoh's dream showed that Egypt would have seven years of plenty to eat. But then seven years would come when the crops would fail and there wouldn't be enough.

Joseph told Pharaoh to save extra food in the first seven years so the nation wouldn't be destroyed by the famine. He wanted to prevent the people from dying of hunger. God used Joseph to save people who would have starved otherwise.

The dream that God sent to Pharaoh was not just for him. The vision was for the sake of normal people, who would suffer most in a famine. God showed his concern for the workers, the moms, the dads, the children. God has mercy on those in need, and we can do the same. We can help the hungry even when God doesn't give us a dream as a warning.

Pharaoh was impressed with Joseph after he explained the dream. He put Joseph in charge of the food. He would be the second-most important person in all of Egypt.

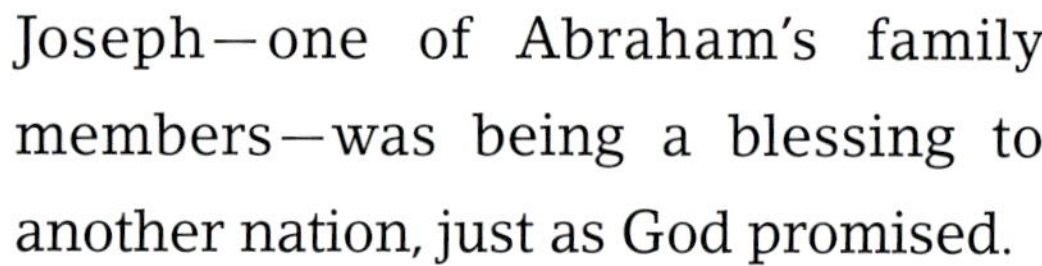

Joseph—one of Abraham's family members—was being a blessing to another nation, just as God promised.

Joseph's brothers had two choices: starvation or a road trip to Egypt. They chose the road trip. When they got to Egypt, who was there to give them the

food they needed to survive? Joseph! But they did not recognize him. Eventually he told them who he was, and the family was reunited.

His brothers were afraid. What if Joseph tried to get revenge on them?

Joseph calmed their fears, saying, "You did a bad thing, but God used that bad thing to save many lives. I see his hand in all that happened to me. Do not be afraid—I will take care of you."

Now for the second family reunion. While Joseph lived in Egypt, he married an Egyptian woman named Asenath. They had two sons, Ephraim and Manasseh. These boys were from two worlds: the Israelite world of their father and the Egyptian world of their mother. Joseph taught them to trust God in a strange land.

Jacob, their grandfather, was dying. Joseph decided to bring his two boys to see their grandfather before he passed away.

Jacob said, "God appeared to me in Canaan. He promised to make me into a large nation. He said this nation would be diverse—made up of people from all over." God first made this promise to Abraham, repeated the promise to Abraham's son Isaac, and then shared it with Isaac's son Jacob. The members of the family changed, but God's promise did not.

Jacob had an idea. He adopted these two half-Egyptian and half-Israelite boys. He made Ephraim and Manasseh the beginning of two of the twelve tribes of Israel.

The story of Ephraim and Manasseh shows us what God's family was always supposed to be: people from every nation gathered to worship God.

EXODUS 1:1–2:10

Jochebed, Puah, and Shiphrah: Some Very Brave Women

The midwives, however, feared God and did not do what the king of Egypt had told them to do; they let the boys live.
Exodus 1:17

God kept his promises to Abraham, Isaac, and Jacob.

While they lived in Egypt, the people of Israel multiplied. Egypt was a powerful empire with lots of money and a big army, but the Egyptians were afraid of how big Israel was becoming.

To stop Abraham's family from growing, Pharaoh enslaved the people of Israel. He forced the Israelites to work hard building cities for Egypt. They suffered long, hot days of toil under a punishing sun. The Egyptian leaders showed no compassion toward Israel.

Too often, people with power use it to get more things for themselves. This hurts people with no one to stand up for them. Pharaoh had power, and Israel did not. But God was with the Israelites. They continued to grow. Pharaoh's hatred was not more powerful than God's love.

Pharaoh decided to do more evil. He had a dark plan to destroy Israel's future. He spoke to Puah and Shiphrah, two women who helped deliver the Israelites' babies. Pharaoh told them, "Kill the boys who are born, but let the girls live."

Puah and Shiphrah had a decision to make. They could keep themselves safe and turn their backs on their people. After all, Pharaoh had power over life and death. He could make things hard for them if they disobeyed—he could even kill them. Puah and Shiphrah probably spent a lot of time in prayer and hushed conversations about what to do. They decided they loved God and their people more than they feared Pharaoh. These women had heart and courage.

Sometimes the people of God must say no to the evil commands of rulers. Puah and Shiphrah may not be as famous as David or Solomon, but there would be no David or Solomon if these ordinary women hadn't shown extraordinary bravery. They were heroes.

During this time, an Israelite woman named Jochebed had a son. She fed him in secret and kept him far away from watching eyes. He was her private joy. But it became too hard to keep him hidden. She needed a new plan.

Jochebed had an idea. Maybe she could get someone to protect her baby. One day, Jochebed and her daughter put the baby in a basket and sent him floating down the river. The basket was made well so the little child would not sink as he bobbed and bounced.

His sister kept watch to see what would happen to her brother. She stood trembling at the edge of the river, both hopeful and afraid to hope.

Their plan worked!

Pharaoh's daughter was bathing in the river when she found the baby crying in his basket. She saw him and had pity.

This was his sister's chance. She ran up to Pharaoh's daughter and said, "I see that you found a Hebrew boy. I know someone who can help you take care of him."

Pharaoh's daughter said, "That sounds like a great idea!"

The boy's sister sprinted home

and told her family, "He has been rescued. Pharaoh's daughter saw him and took him in. And it gets even better. I offered to find someone to take care of the baby. Hurry, Mom, let's go!"

Jochebed must have been shocked and full of joy. She went to meet Pharaoh's daughter and agreed to care for the baby boy.

Pharaoh's daughter decided to raise the boy as her own. She named him Moses.

Moses grew up to do important things for God because of the brave women who risked everything to save the baby boys of Israel.

EXODUS 2:11–12:50

The Exodus: A God of Freedom

I have indeed seen the misery of my people in Egypt.
Exodus 3:7

Moses grew up as part of Pharaoh's family, surrounded by Egyptians. He felt different because he was not like all the other boys and girls around him. He was an Israelite, and he saw how his people were treated. Their pain made him angry.

One day, when Moses was an adult, he saw an Egyptian beating an Israelite slave. The repeated blows and the moans of his fellow Israelite enraged him, so he killed the Egyptian. Moses was right to be upset about the slavery of his people, but he was wrong to try to solve the problem on his own without God's help.

Moses fled from Egypt to an area called Midian. He settled down there and married a woman named Zipporah. He may have given up on helping his people, but God had not.

Moses thought his story would end in failure. But God's specialty is second chances. There is always more grace.

While Moses was in Midian, God's people in Egypt continued to groan under their slavery. They cried to God for help. The good news is that God heard. He remembered the promises he made to Abraham, Isaac, and Jacob.

One afternoon, Moses was tending his father-in-law's sheep when he saw something that would change his life. He saw the angel of the Lord in a flame within a bush. The bush was on fire, but it was not burning up! Moses went to take a closer look.

God called from the bush, "Moses! Moses!"

A shocked Moses answered, "I am here."

God told Moses, "Do not come closer. Take off your shoes—the place where you are standing is holy. I am the God of your fathers, the God of Abraham, Isaac, and Jacob. I have seen how the Egyptians are treating my people, and I have come to set them free. I will take them to a wonderful land that has everything that they need. You must go to Pharaoh to bring my people freedom."

Failure had changed Moses. He did not think he could lead his people, and he was right about that. He could only do it because God would be with him. Moses is not the hero of this story. God is.

Moses wanted to know what to do if the people asked about who sent him. He wanted to know God's name.

God answered, "I AM WHO I AM." That may seem like a strange answer. What does it mean?

God's name means a lot of things. But here it means no one created God. He was here before there was a before. I AM means that God is the beginning of every conversation, the star of every movie, the hero of all our stories. But he also has a name. A name means we can know him. We can be his friend. He is the one who sets slaves free to worship him.

Moses had two problems in Egypt: Pharaoh did not want to let Israel go, and Israel had given up hope. God solved both problems the same way. When the people had no heart left to fight, God fought for them.

God sent plagues on the Egyptians, including locusts, hail, and three days of deep darkness to show that he was all-powerful—and that they must let Israel go. Despite the plagues, Pharaoh refused over and over. Things got worse and worse.

There was one final plague. God ordered Moses to tell Pharaoh that all the firstborn sons in Egypt would die. The Israelites would be spared this sadness if they followed God's instructions. Each family had to offer a lamb as a sacrifice to God. They took the blood from the offering and put it on their doorways. When the Lord sent the punishment to Egypt, he promised to *pass over* his people who did this.

God did pass over the Israelites that night. This is an event the Jewish people remember every year on the Passover holiday.

Pharaoh eventually gave in and let the Israelites go. Other ethnic groups in Egypt saw how powerful the God of Israel was. They saw that he cared about the suffering of slaves. Some of these people decided to leave with Israel, making God's family more diverse.

The story of Moses and Israel has a lot of parts that make us sad. There is a lot of death and evil. There is also a lot of God. He sees when people are hurting—and he helps.

The story of the Exodus—the escape from Egypt—is very important to Israel. It is also important to God. This story helps us understand who God is and what he is like. He is a God who rescues the needy. He is a God who wants a big, diverse family that praises his name.

THE BOOKS OF EXODUS AND DEUTERONOMY

God's Laws and God's Justice

Do not deprive the foreigner or the fatherless of justice.
Deuteronomy 24:17

Why did God rescue his people from slavery in Egypt? He did it to keep his promise to Abraham.

God had promised Abraham that he would give his family a land of their own. Everyone wants to feel safe and at home in a place where they are loved. God wanted that for his people too.

There's also another reason. God rescued Israel from slavery so they could live fully for him. He wanted his people to be an example of life with God so other nations would also want to know God.

But what does living with God look like? How would the Israelites do it? When Moses led the people out of Egypt, they came to Mount Sinai. It was there that God gave Israel the laws that would show them how to worship and obey him.

Every family has rules. Sometimes rules can be frustrating, but they are not bad. They keep us from hurting ourselves and others. It is good news that parents don't let their kids eat candy for breakfast, lunch, and dinner. That might sound great, but it would give us a tummy ache.

God's laws are the same. They keep us from hurting people. They give us ways to say thank you to God by obeying him.

Laws teach us about the Lawgiver. God's laws are a picture of what he wants his people to be.

God's laws paint a picture of a good life.

We can also see God's laws as protection. We are not always kind to one another. Sometimes we do bad things. God's laws helped Israel know what to do when things went wrong.

God made lots of laws about things like worshiping him the right way, telling the truth, honoring parents, and not stealing or hurting people. These laws are important.

A few particular laws clearly point to God's compassionate heart. In the book of Exodus, God warned Israel not to be unkind to people from other countries. The Israelites had been foreigners in Egypt, so they knew what it was like to be outsiders. When the Egyptians saw someone from another country, they used that as a reason to be cruel. God's people were expected to act differently. God expected the Israelites to treat people from other countries fairly.

Hard things happened to Israel. They were slaves for many years. But those hard things were supposed to soften their hearts. That pain helped them to understand how hard it was for other hurting people. When God set his people free from slavery, he showed them the kind of God they served—and he demonstrated what love looks like. God commanded Israel to extend that love to others.

God's compassion is also clear in his laws for the poor. God promised to bless the people of Israel with lots of food if they obeyed his laws. But he had rules about collecting the food. At harvest time, the Israelites were supposed to leave some food in the field or on the tree so that everyone would have enough—especially people who were poor or from a foreign country.

God also wanted to make sure everyone had a fair trial. He warned Israel to show justice to the rich and to the poor. Guilty is guilty. Innocent is innocent. God told judges not to accept money from the rich to buy their freedom. God didn't want people with money and power to use that power to harm other people or to get unfair privileges for themselves.

Do you see the picture God painted with his laws? God wanted his people to worship and obey him. God wanted his people to love each other. God wanted his people to look out for those who are easy to forget.

This was a big job. In Bible times, God's people had a hard time being the kind of people described in his laws. So do we. We are not always kind or honest. We do not always like to share. We do not always like to worship. But that's okay, because there is someone who did all the things we cannot do. He obeyed every single one of God's laws. He is the kind of person God wants us to be, and his life paints a perfect picture of what God is like. But that part of the story is not here yet.

THE BOOK OF JUDGES

Judges: The People Lose Their Way, but God Doesn't

In those days Israel had no king.
Judges 18:1

The people of Israel took over the land God promised them. Long before, God had told Abraham that his descendants would not enter the Promised Land until the people who lived there committed enough sins to lead to judgment. Later in Israel's story, the Israelites would also commit many sins—and be exiled from the land as well. God judges sin no matter who does it, but God also shows grace even when we do not deserve it. The good news is that we do not always get what we deserve.

Israel won many battles against the people who lived in the land—but it wasn't because they were stronger than the other armies. The Israelites usually fought with old, secondhand weapons made from their farm tools. They were often outnumbered, and they had to fight against soldiers with bigger muscles and more practice. But Israel won. Israel won because God helped them.

After Moses died, Joshua replaced him as leader of Israel. Joshua and the people his age remembered the long, hot days in the wilderness. They remembered God giving them food in the desert when they were hungry and water when they were thirsty.

They remembered the stories of how God fought for Israel and freed them from slavery. They remembered God's punishments when their parents worshiped false gods in the wilderness. They remembered and remembered and remembered some more.

God told the Israelites, "These remaining battles are a test to see if you really want to be my people." The test was not about the strength of Israel's army. It was a test of their trust in God. It is easy to trust God when things are good—when we are happy and have food and clothes and a place to live. It is harder to trust God when we do not have all we need.

The time after Joshua died is not a happy part of the story of Israel. All of our stories have sad parts. In this part of the story of Israel, the people stopped trusting God. They decided the false gods other nations worshiped were better than the God who rescued them from slavery.

It is easy to forget the things people do for us. We can forget all the times our siblings let us play with their toys. We only remember when they said no. We can say to our teacher or parent, "You never let me have fun," even though we know it's not true. The people of Israel forgot and forgot and forgot some more.

When they forgot, God gave them what they wanted. He let them go their own way. Going their own way meant other armies defeated them. After all, the Israelites weren't strong apart from God.

These other nations made Israel serve them. Life without God led to more and more pain.

But God loved Israel. He never forgot his promises. And God loves rescuing. It is his joy. When the Israelites cried out to God, asking him to save them, he sent judges to rescue the people. A judge back then was not exactly like a judge today. They did make decisions about arguments between Israelites, but they also fought battles and led the nation.

One time God sent a judge named Deborah to rescue the Israelites. She was a prophetess. That means the Spirit of God helped her understand what God wanted the people to do. The people came to Deborah so she could help them settle their disagreements. She showed them how to obey God's laws.

God told Deborah to speak with a military commander named Barak. He was supposed to lead Israel into battle, but he was afraid to go unless Deborah went too. Deborah agreed to go with him, and Israel won the victory. Israel had peace for forty years because of Deborah.

But then Israel forgot God again. Another nation made them servants, and the people cried out to God yet again. It was like a television show on repeat.

God rescued them over and over. But each time the people forgot God, they drifted further into evil and hurt people who couldn't defend themselves.

Why did they do this? The writer of Judges thinks it was because Israel did not have a king. Without a king to point them to God, the people did what appeared best to them. Sometimes what seems good to us can lead to evil.

God promised Israel that he would send them a king to lead them in the right way. One day, he would send a King from the family of David: Jesus, the Son of God. We haven't met David yet. He is on the way.

But even before God sent the promised King, he did not forget his people. He heard their cries. He sent Deborah and many like her to rescue Israel.

Can we decide for ourselves how we should live? Do we need God, our Maker, to show us what to do? Or do we need a king chosen by God to lead us? The bad things that happened in the time of the judges show that people need God and a king. We need God *as* King. We received just that in a way we never could have expected: through the coming of Jesus, who was fully God and fully human.

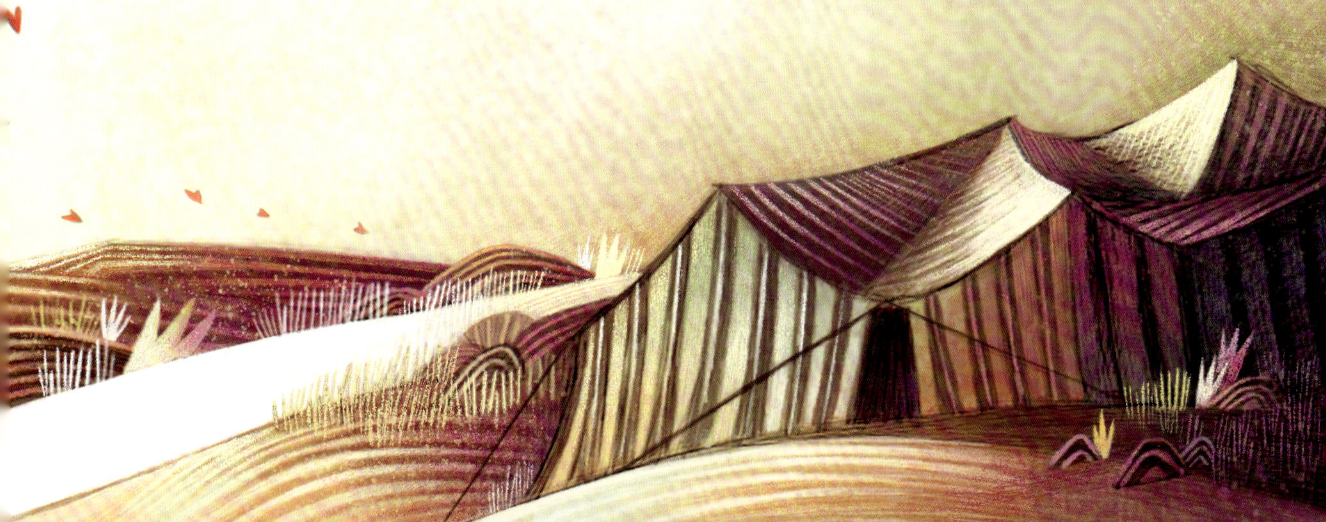

THE BOOK OF RUTH

A Faithful God and a Faithful Friend: The Story of Ruth

Ruth clung to her.
Ruth 1:14

During the time of the judges, a man named Elimelek; his wife, Naomi; and their two sons, Mahlon and Kilion, lived in Bethlehem, a city in Israel. They moved to the land of Moab because there was a famine in Israel. Do you remember when we talked about famines before, in Joseph's story? A famine happens when there is not enough food to feed all the people in a place.

Moab was outside of the land that God promised to Abraham and his family. The people of Israel and the people of Moab did not always get along. But Elimelek decided food in a foreign land was better than death in Israel. The family made a life there. The two sons both married women from Moab, Orpah and Ruth.

But then this sad story got worse. Elimelek, Mahlon, and Kilion died. Now the three women were all widows.

Naomi heard that the famine was over in Israel, and she decided to return to Bethlehem. Her family had gone to a foreign land looking for hope and only found sadness and pain.

She told her two daughters-in-law to return to their people in Moab. Orpah and Ruth cried and hugged Naomi. Orpah agreed to go back to Moab, but Ruth refused to leave Naomi. Ruth loved her too much to abandon her.

Naomi said, "Your sister-in-law is going back to her people and their gods. You should go too!"

But Ruth said, "Don't tell me to leave you. Where you go I will go, and where you live I will live. Your people will be my people. Your God will be my God." Ruth showed that she was committed to Naomi, the people of God, and the God of Israel no matter what.

Naomi and Ruth arrived in Bethlehem at the time of the harvest. Naomi had a relative there named Boaz.

Ruth had an idea. She decided to go to the fields where the grain was being harvested. Remember the law in Israel that the people who harvested the fields must leave some for the poor and the foreigner? Ruth needed this law to provide for herself and Naomi.

Ruth went out to begin a long day of hard work gathering grain. She ended up at the field of Boaz.

When Boaz saw her working in the fields, he asked, "Who is that young woman?"

One of the harvesters replied, "The woman from Moab who came with Naomi."

Boaz told Ruth, "Work in this field only. Stay close to the women who work for me."

"Why are you being so kind to me, a foreign woman?" Ruth asked.

“I heard about how you left your family and your home to come here and be with Naomi,” Boaz answered. “May God bless you for what you did.”

God had provided for them. But there were more provisions coming.

One day Naomi said to Ruth, “My daughter, I must find you a husband to take care of you.”

This may seem strange to us. But life in Bible times was not like it is now. A woman couldn’t just get a job or rent an apartment. She depended on her husband for everything she needed. And Naomi had someone in mind for Ruth: Boaz. He was a good choice because he was honest and kind, and as a relative of Ruth’s deceased husband, he had a legal right to marry her.

Naomi told Ruth to take a bath, put on perfume, and go to Boaz at night when he was sleeping. She was to sneak in and go to sleep at his feet. This was a very tricky thing to do. How would Boaz respond?

Ruth did what Naomi suggested. When Boaz woke up, he said, “What is happening? Who are you?”

Have you ever been surprised when you were woken up in the middle of the night? Then you know how Boaz felt!

Ruth answered, “I am Ruth, your servant. You have a legal right to marry me.” This was very bold. Ruth, a poor foreign woman, goes to Boaz, a rich Israelite, and offers him a chance to get married!

But guess what Boaz said? "God bless you. I will marry you because you are such a noble woman."

Everything went as planned. Boaz and Ruth got married. And once they were married, they had a son named Obed. Obed would one day become the father of Jesse, and Jesse would be the father of David—the future king of Israel.

At first, this may seem like a small story about two women—and it is. But God was in the middle of this small story. He cares about the widow and the foreigner and the people forgotten by the world.

It is also a story about courage, faithfulness, and God's provision. Ruth was a lot like Abraham. She left all that she knew for a future that remained in the hands of God. Like Abraham and Sarah, against all odds she had a son. That son began a line of kings that would produce the one true King, Jesus. The story of Ruth shows us that God's family is big enough to include anybody.

1 SAMUEL 8:4–2 SAMUEL 7:29

David and the God Who Sees Us

The Lord does not look at the things people look at.
People look at the outward appearance,
but the Lord looks at the heart.
1 Samuel 16:7

The story of David's grandfather Obed would not be possible without the story of Ruth—who was from Moab, not Israel. God's family has always been made up of different nations and ethnic groups. But who was David? David was the second king of Israel.

The first king of Israel was named Saul. The Israelite people had asked God for a king like the other nations had. They wanted someone tall, strong, and handsome. They wanted someone who looked like a king and fought like a king.

God had always planned to give Israel a king when they were ready. But they were not ready, and they wanted a king for the wrong reasons. They wanted a king so they could be like the other nations. Trying to be like other nations was rejecting God as king. God decided to do what they wanted anyway. He sent one of his prophets, Samuel, to make Saul king over Israel.

Saul won some battles, but he was not faithful to God. So God took the kingdom away from Saul.

God told Samuel that he had chosen someone to replace Saul. Samuel was sad about Saul's failure. He was also curious about the kind of king God would choose next. He wondered, *How tall and strong will he be? What will he be like? Who will he be?*

God didn't tell Samuel what kind of king to expect. He kept him in suspense. God did tell him that one of the sons of Jesse of Bethlehem would be the next king. When Samuel arrived at the home of Jesse, he saw the oldest son first. His name was Eliab.

Surely, Samuel thought, *this is the one. Eliab is tall and good-looking. He looks like he knows what to do with a sword*.

We are used to thinking that God likes what we like and that God prefers the people we think are best. We assume that God also dislikes the people we dislike. Some people may even be tempted to think that God likes certain races better than others. This is wrong.

We may believe God prefers people who are good at sports or dancing or singing better than less talented people. This is wrong.

We may think God likes people with money more than he likes poor people. This is wrong too.

Samuel was wrong to think that God's view of people was the same as his own view.

God told him, "Do not pay attention to how he looks or how tall he is. That is how humans think. I look at a person's heart." God rejected Eliab. He would not be king. There were a lot more rejections on the way.

Jesse brought out his next son, Abinadab.

God said no. Then Jesse's next son, Shammah, stepped forward. God said no again.

In total, Jesse brought forward seven sons, and God said no to all of them.

Samuel must have thought this trip was a waste of time. He was shocked and then resigned to all the rejections. Ready to give up, he asked Jesse, "Are these all the sons you have?"

"I have one more," Jesse answered cautiously. All the rejections had surprised Jesse. He went from thinking that one of his sons might be king to being humbled by God. But there was still another son, though he was a long shot. "There's the youngest," Jesse said. "He takes care of the sheep."

When David came up, everything changed. God told Samuel, "Go pour oil over the head of this son. He is the one." Samuel did as God told him, and the Spirit of God rushed upon David. The Spirit would help David rule. David was handsome like many of his brothers, but that was not why God chose him. David became king because he had a heart for God.

God's choice of David is important because it shows that we don't have to be the oldest or the biggest to be used by God. God loves to turn those rules upside down.

When David became king, he did some things very well. He was a mighty warrior and a poet. He wrote beautiful songs about God and Israel. But he also used his power as king in ways that did not bring glory to God.

Even though David did bad things, God made a promise to him. He promised David that one of his sons would always rule over Israel. This happened over and over. Some of David's descendants were good kings; some were bad. The successes and failures of these kings led people to dream of a great king who would solve all Israel's problems.

Some said that he would stand up for the poor and needy. Others said he would be the one to bless the non-Jewish nations just as God promised Abraham. Everyone agreed that this king would bring justice and fairness to the world.

God would keep his promises to David. He would send a King who cared about the needy. This King would fulfill all of God's promises to Abraham. David didn't know who the future King would be, but we do. We have met the one the prophets longed to see: Jesus, the promised King. He is here.

THE BOOKS OF 1 AND 2 KINGS

The Kings of Israel: Failure and Hope

Observe what the Lord your God requires: Walk in obedience to him, and keep his decrees and commands, his laws and regulations, as written in the Law of Moses. Do this so that you may prosper in all you do and wherever you go.

1 Kings 2:3

David's son Solomon became the next king of Israel. Being a king is a hard job, and being the king in charge of God's people might have been the hardest job in the world. Solomon needed advice, so David gave it to him. Parents are supposed to teach their kids the things they've learned about life. David gave Solomon lots of advice, but it all boiled down to this: "Be strong and have courage. Listen to the Lord. Obey the laws that God gave to Moses. If you do this, everything will turn out okay."

Solomon valued this advice. And he realized that God knew even more than his father about what it would take to be a good king. *There are lots of people giving me advice about how to live,* Solomon thought. *Being the leader of God's people means trusting that God knows best.* So he asked God to give him wisdom, and God did just that.

What did God say in his laws about being a king?

Solomon read that the king should serve the people, not expect the people to serve him. He should not buy too many horses or try to get all the silver or gold. He should keep the book of God's law close. He should read it every day.

There was more to being the king than just reading the rules about being king. Solomon saw that he had to follow and obey God like everyone else in Israel.

In his law, God reminds his people over and over again to worship and trust him alone. Does God need our worship? No, but we tend to become like what we worship. When God is our hero, we become more and more like him. What could be better?

Solomon also read about God's compassion for the poor and the needy. Since the king had lots of power, he could make sure people were treated fairly.

It was all in the book of God's law. God knew that the king's behavior would impact the nation's behavior. It is just like at your home. You probably go to church because your parent, grandparent, or caregiver takes you there. Before you could read, you needed someone to read the Bible to you. We all need someone to point us to God. But no parent can point their children to God unless they know him first. The king was like the parent of the whole country of Israel. It was his job to point everyone to God.

Solomon did some good things. He used his wisdom to help people settle their disagreements. He built a Temple so the people

could worship God there. But he also built a big house for himself. He loved power and money more than God. He made the people his servants instead of serving the people, and—worst of all—he worshiped false gods.

Solomon was not the only king of Israel who did not follow God's law completely. Many of the kings worshiped other gods and let the rest of the nation do the same.

A few kings did obey God, though. One king who followed God's rules was named Josiah. When he was king, the people found the book of God's law. It had been lost at some point, and the kings had not been reading it.

When Josiah heard all that was written in the law, he was heart-broken. He said, "I know that Israel has not been obeying the law, but we need to start now." He asked the priests, "What will happen to us if we keep ignoring God's laws?"

The priests told Josiah, "God will punish us if we ignore his laws, but since you have turned back to him, God will not judge Israel while you are king."

Josiah knew what he had to do. For the rest of his life, he made it his goal to point Israel toward God.

I wish I could say that the kings who followed him did the same thing. But they did not.

They kept worshiping false gods and taking advantage of the people. God sent prophets to warn Israel and the kings about what would happen if they did not change their ways, but the people did not want to change. The kings did not want to change. After over four hundred years of Israel's refusal to change, God judged them for their sins.

God was very patient. He did not judge the Israelites for their first or even their one hundredth sin, but he did judge them eventually. He allowed a foreign nation, Babylon, to come into Israel and destroy the Temple. This was one of the saddest events in the history of Israel. The Temple—where they had gathered to meet with God, worship him, and offer him sacrifices—was burned down. The homes and gardens the people had built were destroyed.

The Israelites had to move to a foreign country and serve the people there. But even then, God promised that one day he would bring them back to the land he had given them. Because God always keeps his promises, the people had hope.

THE BOOK OF ISAIAH

The Prophet Isaiah and God's Important Mission

I heard the voice of the Lord saying,
"Whom shall I send? And who will go for us?"
And I said, "Here am I. Send me!"
Isaiah 6:8

I forget things all the time. I forget important things and silly things. I forget where I left my favorite sweater. Once I forgot my sister's birthday (sorry, Tasha). The Israelites forgot how to live as God's people. Well, they either forgot or they just stopped doing what God asked them to do. When Israel forgot or ignored God, he sent prophets to remind them what it meant to live for him.

These prophets were inspired by God's Spirit to tell Israel the truth about what God wanted. God's Spirit also showed them what God had planned for their future. In this future, Israel would obey God and a just King would rule.

Prophets had a hard job—maybe even harder than the king's job. They had to tell the people when they were wrong. No one likes to be told they are wrong. But the prophets loved the Israelites enough to tell them that they could be better.

God called a prophet named Isaiah to help the Israelites remember all the things they had forgotten.

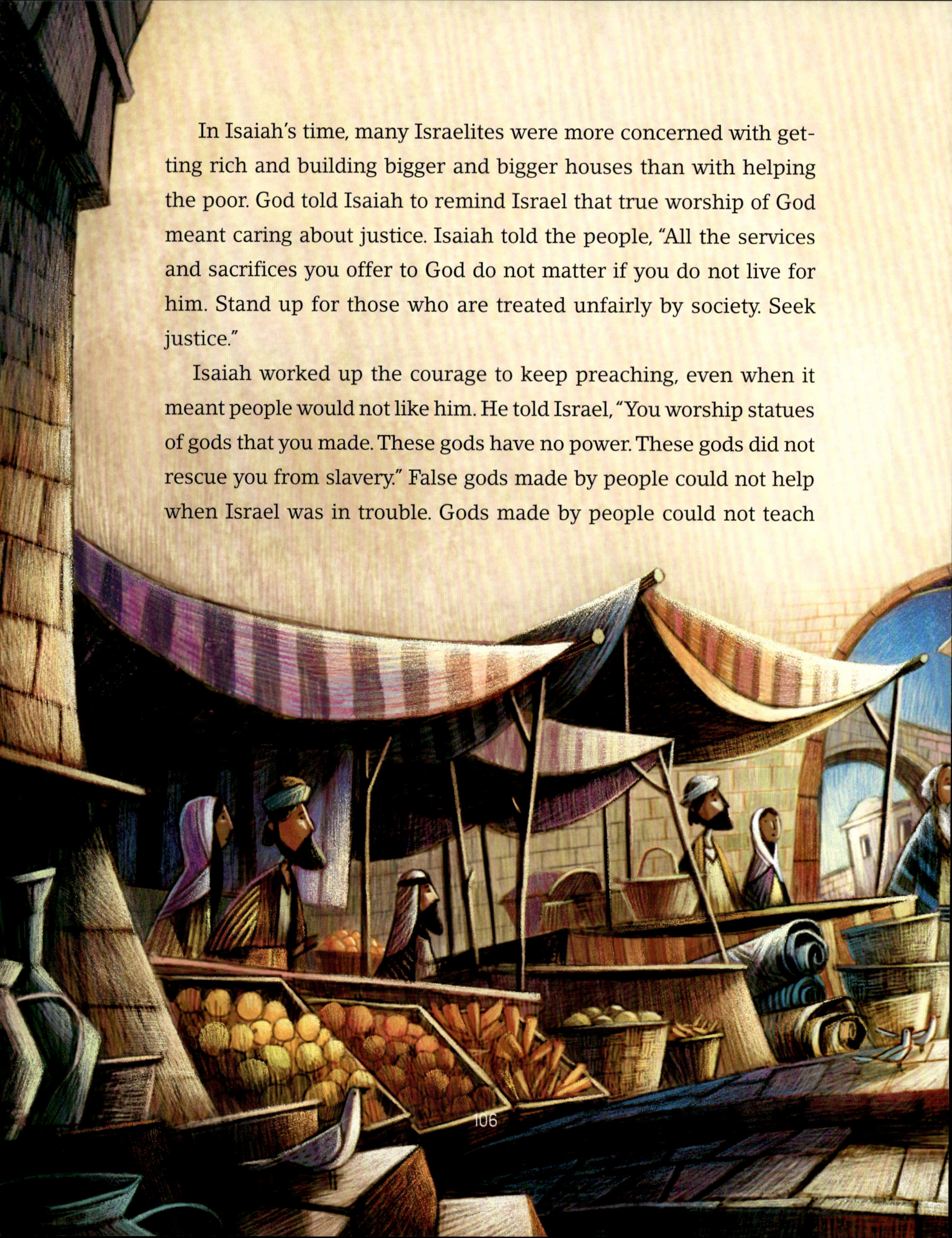

In Isaiah's time, many Israelites were more concerned with getting rich and building bigger and bigger houses than with helping the poor. God told Isaiah to remind Israel that true worship of God meant caring about justice. Isaiah told the people, "All the services and sacrifices you offer to God do not matter if you do not live for him. Stand up for those who are treated unfairly by society. Seek justice."

Isaiah worked up the courage to keep preaching, even when it meant people would not like him. He told Israel, "You worship statues of gods that you made. These gods have no power. These gods did not rescue you from slavery." False gods made by people could not help when Israel was in trouble. Gods made by people could not teach

Israel how to live. Gods made by people led to pain, and God didn't want his people to be hurt.

Isaiah went to the towns, marketplaces, courthouses, and fancy neighborhoods in Israel and said, "Stop taking bribes. Stop caring so much about your own comfort. Stop living for yourselves alone."

God gave Isaiah a really hard question to ask the Israelites: "Why are you hurting my people and making things hard for the poor?"

Isaiah knew the people would not listen. They would go into exile in spite of all his efforts to turn them around, but God's Spirit helped Isaiah remember that the judgment of exile was not the end. Isaiah looked forward to a time when God would remember his promises to Abraham.

Isaiah told the people that one day God would bring an end to their suffering and allow them to return to the Promised Land.

Isaiah also spoke about a servant, chosen by God, who would arrive on the scene someday. He would restore Israel, but he would have an even bigger job than that. God told Isaiah, "I will do more than just restore the Twelve Tribes of Israel. I will make Israel a light to all the nations. Then my salvation will reach the whole world." God's plan was to rescue people from every nation on the planet. Whether your skin is brown or black or white or somewhere in between, if you are on the planet, you are a part of God's plan.

Isaiah spoke about two characters who would be part of God's real-life drama someday: the King and the one who suffers. Isaiah said an amazing King would come from David's family. God's Spirit would give him wisdom and strength. This King would not be like the kings who only cared about themselves.

Isaiah said, "When this King rules, the wolf will live with the lamb and the leopard will lie down with the goat." Normally, a lamb would be a wolf's dinner. That is how different this future King would make things.

The job of the other character was much sadder. Isaiah called him a man of suffering. This man would carry the sufferings of the people. Isaiah said the man of suffering would be pierced for *our sins* and crushed for the things *we did wrong*.

What does all this mean? I am not sure that even Isaiah understood fully. Isaiah was in the land of mysteries, carried there by God's Spirit. But it turns out the man of suffering and the King were the same person. Jesus in his life would be both. He is the one who suffered for our sins and the one who rules.

Isaiah leaves us with stories and pictures of justice, living for God, a King, and a Kingdom. He leaves us with stories of one who suffers. Not until Jesus came would all these stories weave together into one story, and God's picture would finally become clear.

THE BOOK OF DANIEL

Daniel and His Friends: God Is with Us No Matter Where We Go

Praise be to the name of God for ever and ever;
wisdom and power are his. He changes times and seasons;
he deposes kings and raises up others. He gives wisdom
to the wise and knowledge to the discerning.
Daniel 2:20-21

It is easy to follow God when everything is going well.

Daniel and his friends Shadrach, Meshach, and Abednego had to live for God when things were hard. When the Babylonians took over Israel, they carried away many of the people into exile. These four young men grew up in a foreign land away from friends and family.

The Babylonians assigned Daniel, Shadrach, Meshach, and Abednego to serve the king. They wanted to make Daniel and his friends live like them. They tried to give them food that was against God's law to eat. But Daniel decided to follow God even if it got him in trouble.

Daniel asked his guard, "Can we just eat vegetables instead of the royal food?" The guard allowed it, and Daniel and his friends became healthier than those who ate the Babylonian diet.

The king of Babylon was named Nebuchadnezzar. He believed that his money and power made him a god. Nebuchadnezzar designed a huge statue of himself and made a law that said, "When a certain kind of music is played, everyone must bow down to worship my image. If you do not, you will be sentenced to die in a fiery furnace."

Everyone obeyed except a brave few. Guess who they were?

The king received a report: "Shadrach, Meshach, and Abednego are not following your law. As a matter of fact, these Jewish people do not worship our gods at all."

Nebuchadnezzar was furious. Who did these young men think they were to defy him? In a rage, he had them brought to him. He said, "Is it true that you refuse to worship our gods or the statue I created? You have two choices: worship my statue or be thrown into the fiery furnace."

Full of God-given courage, Shadrach, Meshach, and Abednego answered the king. "If you throw us into the fire, God can save us—but even if he does not, we still will not worship your gods or the image you put up."

Their refusal made the king even angrier. He ordered the three of them to be tied up and tossed into the fire.

Then the king saw something that shocked him. He said to his officials, "Didn't we put three men in the fire? Why do I see a fourth man in the fire who looks like a son of the gods?"

The king was correct. Someone was with the three men. God didn't prevent them from facing this hard thing, but he was with them through it.

Nebuchadnezzar shouted, "Shadrach, Meshach, and Abednego, servants of the Most High God, come out!"

The crowd was amazed that the men had not been hurt by the fire. When the king saw that the one true God had saved them, he passed a new law. Now the Jewish people would be free to worship God.

Another time, King Nebuchadnezzar had a dream. It was not the normal kind of strange dream we might have after we watch a movie too scary for us or eat too much late-night pizza. This was a dream from God. The king wanted to know the meaning of the dream. He asked all the people around him, but none could answer, so they brought in Daniel. God had blessed Daniel with the ability to interpret dreams. He had done this for the king before.

Nebuchadnezzar had dreamed about a large tree that grew to the heavens. Its branches spread all over the world. But then a command came from heaven: "Cut the tree down, but let its stump remain in the ground. Let rain fall on him and let him live with animals, and let his mind be changed for a time."

Daniel told Nebuchadnezzar, "You are the tree. You will lose your kingdom for a while until you acknowledge that God is in control. Stop sinning. Do what is right, and be kind to the oppressed. If you do this, God may have mercy on you."

The king did not listen to Daniel, and God did what he showed in the dream. Nebuchadnezzar went crazy until he recognized that God has more power than kings. Those on the wrong side of justice find themselves on the wrong side of God. That is not a good place to be.

God gave Daniel one final gift: a vision of the future. In this vision, Daniel saw a King who would receive a Kingdom that covers the whole world. Because God would choose this King, he would rule rightly. In Daniel's vision, though, the people worshiped the King. But we just saw that Daniel and his friends refused to worship human rulers. Who is this King deserving of worship?

The answer to that question is Jesus: the man who is also God. He would receive worship and rule the world in the right way. But even before he came to earth, God was at work in the lives of his people—including Daniel and his friends.

Sing to the God Who Made Us!

Let Israel rejoice in their Maker;
let the people of Zion be glad in their King.
Psalm 149:2

People love to sing. Different songs are made for different things—for example, we don't sing Christmas songs at birthday parties (unless Christmas is your birthday). Some songs are good for dancing fast, and some songs are good for dancing slow. Some songs are happy, and some songs are sad. Songs are as different as we are.

The people of Israel, especially King David, wrote songs to God called psalms. Because they were written to God, they are both songs and prayers. These songs were used at home and at the Temple and on the roads and in the market. And we still sing and pray them in all sorts of places today!

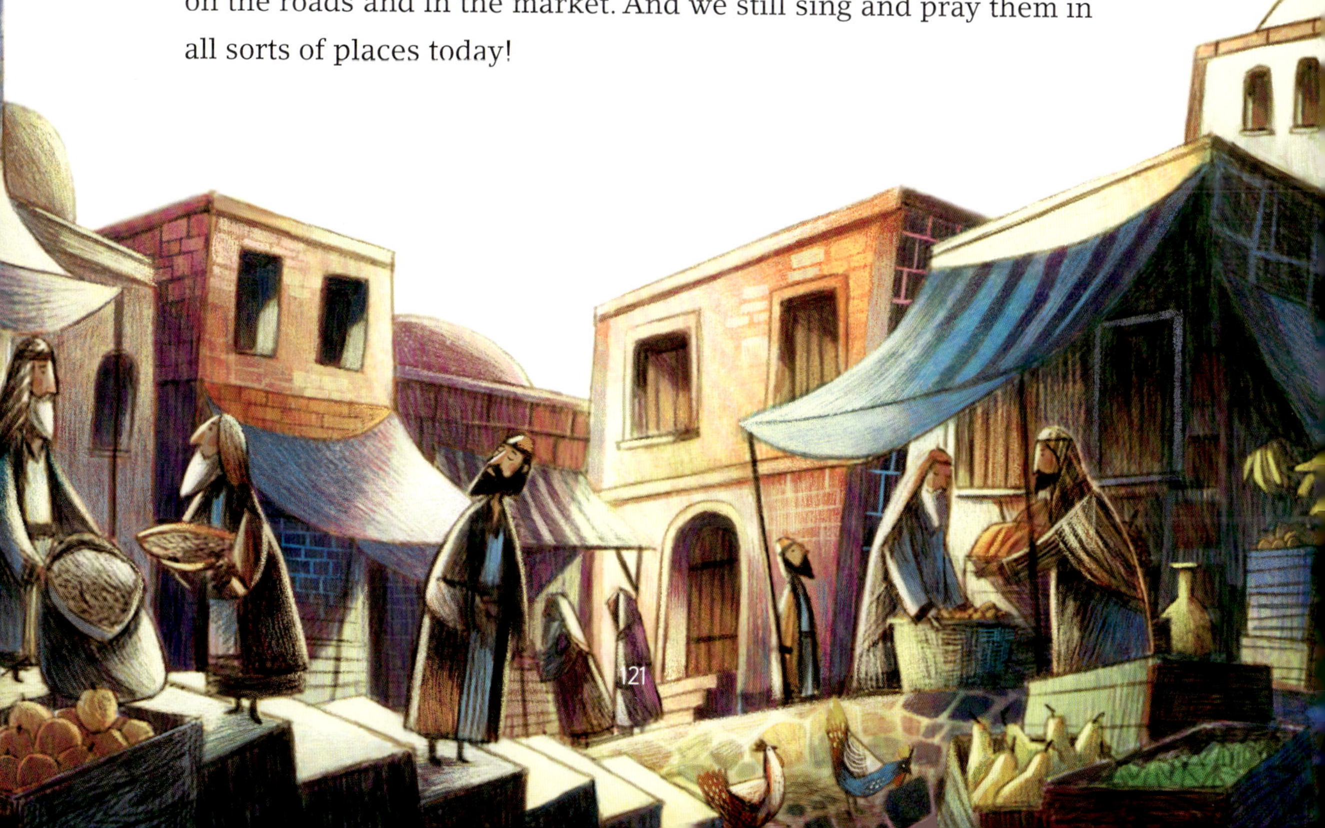

Some psalms taught God's people how to live. Psalm 1 says something like, "Happy is the person who does not hang out with evil people but delights in God's law." The Psalms begin this way because they're intended to remind the people of God to live for God. The best way to live for God is to enjoy and obey the Scriptures that he has given us.

Other psalms praise God for who he is and what he has done. Psalm 100 says, "Shout for joy to the Lord, all the earth. . . . It is he who made us, and we are his!" What is so awesome about God? The fact that he made everything, including you and me!

The people of Israel loved to praise God for creating the world and rescuing them from slavery. We, too, can sing to God for the beautiful world he has made and the things he has done for us. We can trust that the God strong enough to make the world is strong enough to guide us—and we can praise him for that.

The Psalms also talk about bad times. Psalm 42 says, "My tears have been my food day and night, while people say to me all day long, 'Where is your God?'" Life hurts, even when we know God is with us. He wants us to offer that hurt to him. As long as we are crying to God, even our tears can be a prayer. There are more sad songs in the Bible than happy songs.

In the Psalms, we hear about God as the champion of the poor and needy. Psalm 12 says something like this: "'Because the poor are robbed and the needy groan, I will come and help,' says the Lord. 'I will give them the safety they need.'" When there is no one to turn to for help, God steps in.

That's why Psalm 35 says, "My whole being will exclaim, 'Who is like you, Lord? You rescue the poor from those too strong for them, the poor and needy from those who rob them.'" We do not have to be strong. We can know the one who is strong.

Psalms like these help us understand how God feels. He is a God who cares. He sees the hungry and those who do not receive justice, and he steps in and fights for them. When we stand up for the poor and needy, we are being like God. We are showing people God's compassion.

The book of Psalms is a gift to us. It shows us that all of our life—the good and the bad—can be offered to God. We do not have to keep secrets from God because he knows the truth anyway. When we are sad, we can tell God. When we are being bullied and need rescue, we can tell God. When we are happy, we can tell God. No matter how we feel, we can sing with the voices God gave us.

A Pause . . .

We have met many people from the Bible, but the story is not done. The most important person we've met is God. He is the hero of this story. He made the world for us to live in. He made it good, and diversity is part of that goodness. But sin entered the world. Now pain and joy are mixed together.

God has always had a vision to bring together a family of people from every nation in the world. He wants all of us—black, brown, or white—to be with him and to know him. He wants people from Africa, Australia, Asia, and everywhere in between. He doesn't love one group of people more than any other.

Remember God's promise to Abraham? He promised Abraham a place, a land to call his home. He promised to make him the father of many nations. All the people of the world would be blessed through Abraham and his family.

God kept his promise. He added different people from different nations to Abraham's family. Israel became diverse along the way.

Then God gave his people the laws. These laws were good. They taught the people how to worship God and how to live for him. These laws showed that God cared how his people treated others. He loves justice. The poor and needy have a friend in God.

But things didn't go so well for the Israelites. Often, the people of Israel did not keep God's laws. They did not remain faithful to him. They mistreated each other. The rich took advantage of the poor. People lied and cheated. These bad things happened because sin was in them and in the world causing problems. It was not just Israel that sinned. Everyone did. Everyone was in need of a Savior. They needed Jesus, and so do we.

Even Israel's kings failed to follow God. They were sinners too.

God sent the prophets to warn Israel, but the people did not listen.

God judged his people by sending them into exile. But God also promised to bring them back to their home. God's grace and forgiveness was good news for the Israelites back then, and it is still good news for us today!

God did bring the Israelites back to their land, but they still were not free because foreign nations ruled them in their own country. The story was unfinished.

Running through this whole story is a vision of a King and a Kingdom. The Savior King who would come from David's family would rule in the right way. He would lead the people to keep God's laws. All the nations of the world would be blessed by this King. His Kingdom would cover the whole earth one day. He would be a friend to those who were hurting, a champion of those who were weak.

This King has been in the shadows. Now it is time for him to come into the light.

LUKE 1:26-79

Mary and the God Who Turns Things Upside Down

[The Lord] has brought down rulers from their thrones but has lifted up the humble. He has filled the hungry with good things but has sent the rich away empty.

Luke 1:52-53

The story of God and his plan for the world is the biggest and grandest story. In truth, it is the only story, and we are all living in it. This very big story has turning points. There are moments when the big story gets very small. Remember when God appeared to Abraham and told him that his family would bless the whole world? The story got small then.

Now we're going to read about another turning point where God called someone to a very important job. This person was a young woman named Mary.

Mary lived in a small town in Israel called Nazareth. She was a normal girl with normal dreams. She wanted to worship God and make a life with her future husband, Joseph. Sometimes God calls normal people to do big things.

One day, God sent the angel Gabriel to visit Mary. (The name Gabriel means "God is a warrior." What a cool name for an angel.)

"Rejoice, you who are highly favored by God!" Gabriel said. "The Lord is with you!"

Mary was troubled by what Gabriel said and wondered what his words meant. What would make her favored by God? She was a poor girl in a small town in the middle of nowhere.

Gabriel knew that he had worried Mary, so he told her, "Do not be afraid!" (That was easy for Gabriel to say—he was the angel, not the one meeting the angel!)

Gabriel explained, "Mary, you have found favor with God. You will become pregnant and give birth to a son. You will name him Jesus. He will be called the Son of the Most High. God will give him the kingdom of his father David. He will reign forever, and his Kingdom will never end."

This is the Kingdom and family God has been working toward since the beginning! It is a Kingdom that invites everyone to join. Whether you're rich or poor, young or old—no matter where you were born or the color of your skin—God's Kingdom welcomes you.

Gabriel had just given Mary the biggest news in human history. The promised King who would bless and rule the nations would be her son.

She was blessed and favored indeed!

But Mary had an important question: "How can this happen if I'm not married?"

Gabriel answered, "Your child will be a miracle created within your womb when the Spirit of God overshadows you."

Jesus, born of the Spirit and Mary, would be fully human and fully God. He is a walking mystery: God in human flesh.

While Mary pondered this miracle, Gabriel told her about another marvel. "Your relative Elizabeth is also pregnant, despite her old age. Nothing is impossible with God."

Mary's life was changing, and she needed someone to talk to. She decided to go to the only person who would understand: Elizabeth, who was about to have her own miracle baby.

When Mary's feet crossed the entry to Elizabeth's home, the baby in Elizabeth's belly leaped for joy. His was the first of many hearts that Jesus filled with happiness.

Elizabeth, filled with the Spirit, said, "You are a very blessed woman, and your child is blessed too. You are blessed because you believed what God told you."

All of a sudden, we are in a musical. Mary sang the following hymn to mark the occasion:

My soul boasts in the Lord
and my spirit rejoices in God my Savior,
because he cares about me even though I am ordinary and poor.
From now on all generations will remember me as blessed
because God has done great things for me,
and his name is holy.
He shows mercy toward people who fear him in every generation.
With his powerful arm, he has done great things;
He has defeated those with arrogant plans that they made up themselves.
God has taken down the powerful;
God has lifted up the people without power who trust in him.
He has given food to the hungry;
He has sent the rich away with nothing.
He has remembered all the promises he made to Abraham and his family forever.

When God does great things in our lives, it is okay to sing. We can sing at church and at home and in the car. Songs are a way of remembering and praising.

Mary knew it was important that God chose *her*. God didn't choose someone rich or powerful to raise his Son. God doesn't need powerful people to get things done—he has more than enough strength. Mary's song reminds us that God does the opposite of what we expect all the time. He lifts up the poor, and he takes down those who believe they are stronger or wiser than God. Mary worshiped God because he keeps promises and loves justice. We worship him for those exact same reasons today.

LUKE 2:1-20; MATTHEW 1:18–2:12

The Savior Is Here: The Birth of the Messiah

I bring you good news that will cause great joy for all the people. Today in the town of David a Savior has been born to you; he is the Messiah, the Lord.
Luke 2:10-11

When it was almost time for Mary to give birth to Jesus, Caesar Augustus, the ruler of Rome, had an idea. He decided to count all of his subjects. This included Mary and Joseph. Joseph was from the family of David, so he and Mary had to leave Nazareth and travel to Bethlehem—David's hometown—to be counted.

Caesar Augustus's authority to make Mary and the baby Jesus inside her move from one place to another may seem to suggest that Augustus was more powerful than Jesus. That would be wrong. Long ago, God told prophets that the King of his people would be born in Bethlehem. By making Mary travel to Bethlehem, Augustus was helping to make God's plan happen without realizing it.

Jesus was not born in a fancy palace. He was not surrounded by kings and servants. His first meal did not come from a silver spoon. Jesus was born surrounded by animals and regular people. His first bed did not have a fluffy pillow stuffed with feathers. Instead, he slept in a feeding trough. The most powerful being in the whole world—the Son of God—was a helpless babe who relied on his mother to meet all his needs.

God came close to us so that we could come close to him, no matter how ordinary we feel. And whom did God invite to celebrate the birth of his Son? Even more regular people.

On the night that Jesus was born, some shepherds were up late taking care of their flocks. Shepherds were like the cooks, car-repair people, cleaners, or fast-food restaurant workers of their time. Shepherds didn't get invited to the parties for the rich and the famous. They weren't the first ones chosen for sports teams.

But God chose them to participate in the most important celebration ever: the day Jesus was born.

An angel of the Lord appeared to the shepherds. The glory of the Lord shone all around them. They were terrified.

Again, angels: wonderful, but scary.

The angel told them, "Do not be afraid. I bring good news. Today, in David's city, a Savior has been born—the Messiah, the Lord! This will be the sign: you will find the baby wrapped in cloths and lying in a feeding trough."

The shepherds were amazed. What kind of King and Savior would be sleeping in a place used to feed animals? The kind of King who knows and cares about people who struggle to find food and justice. The kind of King with a heart open to the world.

Then the music broke out. Alongside the angel, a heavenly choir sang:

Glory to God in the highest,
and peace on earth among people who receive his favor.

The shepherds found Jesus just as the angel had told them.

A few years later, Jesus and his family received more visitors. These visitors were not shepherds. They were magi—also known as wise men—from a far country east of Israel, and they had been led to Bethlehem by a star. They came to worship the King of the Jews. When they found him, they gave him gifts of gold, perfume, and spices.

Lots of people saw Jesus in those days. Why does the Bible tell the story of people coming from a distant country to see him? This part of the story reminds us what the big story is all about. God's plan was never only for Israelites but for the whole world. The magi were the first people from outside of Israel to seek Jesus. They were not the last. God still brings people from afar to meet and worship his Son.

When Jesus arrived, he was surrounded by his family, animals, and shepherds. He was visited by foreigners and strangers. But no one has to be a stranger or a foreigner to God. He is a God for the people who feel stepped on and ignored. He is with us.

LUKE 2:25-38

Simeon and Anna Meet the Messiah

My eyes have seen your salvation, which you have prepared in the sight of all nations.
Luke 2:30-31

Mary and Joseph loved God and spent lots of time worshiping him. They really liked going to all the festivals of Israel. As they traveled back and forth along the dusty roads from Nazareth to Jerusalem, they sang psalms and recounted the stories of the great victories that God won for his people.

When Jesus was a baby, he didn't understand these songs. He was comforted by them like lullabies that usher us into dreamland.

Jesus' first visit to the Temple came forty days after he was born. Joseph and Mary brought Jesus to present him to the Lord. They gave the offering that the law required after a baby was born. Different people gave different types of offerings. Richer families gave larger animals, but Joseph and Mary gave an offering of two doves. This was the offering for those who could not afford to give anything more. Mary and Joseph were not rich, but they gave what they had. What they gave made God happy. God chose faithful parents to raise his Son.

At the Temple, there was an old man named Simeon. He had a big, bushy gray beard and the kind of voice that made all the little

children feel safe and warm. He would talk to anyone who would listen in the market or the neighborhood about God and his promises. He told the youth to remember Abraham and Sarah, Isaac, Daniel, David, Naomi, and Ruth.

"God will keep his promises. You have to trust him. He is good," Simeon would say.

God had made a promise to Simeon. God told him that he would not die until he saw the Messiah, the promised King.

Simeon wondered, *When will this promise come true? My beard can't get much grayer and my knees can't ache more in the mornings than they already do.* But Simeon never lost faith. He believed what he told other people: "God always keeps his promises."

Simeon was right. One ordinary day, the Holy Spirit prompted Simeon to go to the Temple. And who did he meet? Jesus! When his eyes fell upon the baby, Simeon knew. His whole insides leaped for joy. Sometimes when your heart is full, the only thing you can do is sing. This is the song that Simeon sang:

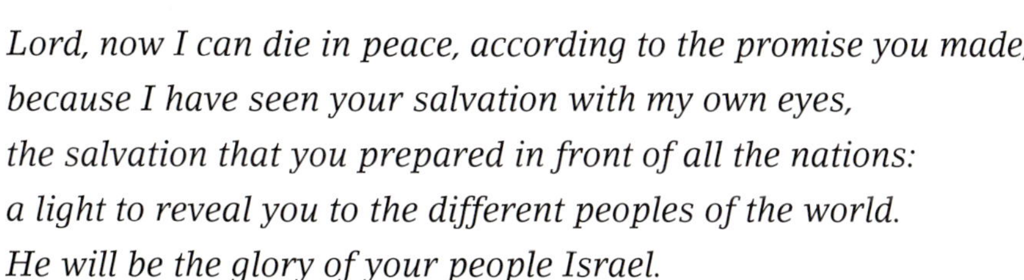

Lord, now I can die in peace, according to the promise you made,
because I have seen your salvation with my own eyes,
the salvation that you prepared in front of all the nations:
a light to reveal you to the different peoples of the world.
He will be the glory of your people Israel.

Simeon did not fear death because he had seen God's salvation. Simeon had met Jesus. Nothing could bother him. When life gets scary for us, we can remember that we are like Simeon. We have not held the baby Jesus in our arms, but we do know him. Nothing can take that away from us.

Simeon was overjoyed because he knew that God's King would bring salvation to the Gentiles. Gentiles were the people in Bible times who weren't Israelites. Simeon knew God's plan was big enough to include all the nations of the world. Jesus would be the glory of Israel because he would bring salvation to all who believed in him.

Another person noticed Jesus at the Temple that day. Her name was Anna. She had long gray hair full of curls. Her voice was rich and always tinged with a hint of laughter, like there was a joke that only she knew. But her joy had not come easy. It was a hard-won thing. She had found joy after going through something very sad. Anna's husband had died long ago, and she had been a widow for many years. She'd spent those years worshiping God, praying, and fasting. We, too, can find joy in God even after the sad things.

When Anna saw baby Jesus, she knew how important he was—just like Simeon did. She began to tell everyone she knew, "I have seen the child of promise. There is hope still left in the world, glory still left in it. God is still with us."

Both Simeon and Anna told people about Jesus after they encountered him. God uses all of us—boys and girls, men and women—to tell the world the story about his Son. It is a story that burst from Israel to the whole world. It made its way all the way from Jerusalem to you and me.

LUKE 3:1-18; MATTHEW 11:1-6

John the Baptist Gets People Ready for Jesus

Every valley shall be filled in, every mountain and hill made low.
The crooked roads shall become straight, the rough ways smooth.
And all people will see God's salvation.
Luke 3:5-6

God told John the Baptist to get everyone ready for Jesus' ministry. (We first met John when he was a baby. He was the child who jumped in Elizabeth's womb when Mary visited her.) Getting everyone ready is not easy. In my house, getting ready for school takes a lot. Everyone has to get dressed, eat breakfast, and find their socks and shoes—and there is always at least one missing sock or shoe!

Getting ready for Jesus to come was not about having the right clothes. It was about having the right heart. To get the people of Israel ready, John led some of them to the desert. Why the desert? Because after God freed his people from slavery, he led them through the wilderness. Going to the wilderness was supposed to remind them that God had rescued them before, and he could do it again.

The wilderness is a dangerous place. It is hot, and there is not a lot of water. Wild animals out there can hurt you. In the wilderness, you need help to survive. Going to the wilderness also reminded the people that they needed God to survive.

John told the people to prepare for Jesus by getting baptized. Baptism showed that they wanted God to wash their sins away. He also said the people must repent. *Repent* is a fancy word that means to turn away from sin and toward God.

Then John preached about the importance of fair treatment. He said, "God is not happy with how you are treating others."

The people asked, "What should we do?"

John said, "If you have two shirts, give one to someone who doesn't have one. If you have food and someone else does not, give them some."

The tax collectors asked, "What should we do?"

John said, "Don't take extra money from the people."

Even the soldiers got into it. They asked, "What should we do?"

John answered, "Don't pressure people to give you money. Don't tell lies about people."

All of this advice had a theme. God cares about how we treat other people. In God's Kingdom, we must treat each other well.

The people liked John. He could have set himself up as king. He could have made people think that he was Israel's hope. John did not do that. He pointed to someone greater. Standing in front of the crowd at the edge of the river, John told them, "Someone way more important than me is on the way. I do not compare to him!"

John was talking about Jesus, of course. He thought that when Jesus came, Israel's problems would go away. But they did not. John got put in jail *after* Jesus showed up. He was confused. *How can things still be hard now that Jesus is here?*

John sent some of his followers to ask Jesus a few questions. "If you are the promised King, why is John in jail? Why aren't God's enemies all defeated? Should we look for another hope?"

Jesus told John's followers, "Spend the day with me. I want to show you what my Kingdom looks like."

There was a sick person on the verge of death. His family had given up hope. His children were weeping. Jesus healed the man.

There was a blind man begging for enough money to buy a meal to make it through the cold Judean night. Jesus healed him too.

There was a woman with an evil spirit that harassed her. Jesus cast out the evil spirit.

John's followers saw all of this and were shocked to silence, awed by what God had done.

Jesus said, "Go tell John what you have seen. The blind see, the lame walk, and the good news is preached to the poor."

Jesus showed John that his Kingdom wasn't about the rich or the powerful. It wasn't about being a warrior like David. Jesus' Kingdom was about healing the hurting people of the world. It was about God's love. It was about the chance to repent and start over.

This was different from what many people expected. But Jesus as King would care about the people everyone forgot: the sick, the hurting, the poor.

Jesus knew that the biggest enemy was not other people. It was the sin that causes people to harm each other. It was the sin that brings death. That was what Jesus came to fight. He would fight for us and win.

LUKE 4:16-21

Jesus' First Sermon at Nazareth

The Spirit of the Lord is on me, because he has anointed me to proclaim good news to the poor.
Luke 4:18

When babies are on the way, families get things ready. We paint the room the new baby will move into. We buy toys, diapers, and clothes. If there is an older sister or brother, we talk to them about the changes the baby will bring.

Jesus grew up in a family surrounded by love. He studied the Jewish Scriptures and went to the festivals that told Israel's story. He prayed and talked to God. Soon it was time for him to begin the work God, his Father, had given him to do.

One Sabbath day, Jesus went to the synagogue in Nazareth. A synagogue was a place where the Jewish people gathered to read Scripture and talk about it.

Jesus stood to read from God's Word, and he was handed the book of Isaiah. All the people in the synagogue fixed their eyes on Jesus. What would he say? What would he do?

Jesus could have chosen any passage to help people understand the work God had prepared for him. Which passage would he choose? What would he say?

After scanning the scroll, Jesus found his text. Full of confidence and conviction, he read, "The Spirit of the Lord is upon me." Jesus would not do his ministry by himself. He would have God's Spirit to help him. All who believe in Jesus have the same Spirit to help us. We are never alone. Good start!

Jesus continued, "He has poured oil over me to preach good news to the poor." Why oil on his head? That was one way of showing that someone had been chosen for a special job—remember when Samuel poured oil over David? In a similar way, God poured his Spirit upon his Son. What was Jesus chosen to do? He was chosen to "preach good news to the poor"!

Who does Jesus mention first? The people who are easy to forget: the poor and needy. What is the good news to the poor? The good news to the poor is the Kingdom of God.

Jesus' coming meant that God's reign as King was beginning on earth. In this Kingdom, there would be justice and righteousness. Instead of getting tricked and robbed, people would be treated fairly.

The arrival of God's Kingdom meant that forgiveness and a new start at life was possible. No matter what sins people had committed, anyone could change and become new! Sign me up for that good news.

Jesus kept reading, voice unwavering, the crowd hanging on every syllable. He said, "God sent me to tell the prisoners they will be set free and to give sight to the blind. God sent me to set free the people who are pressed down by the world. He sent me to let everyone know this is the year of the Lord's favor!"

Jesus' words were like a cool cup of water for people thirsty after a day in the sun. He reminded the people that God saw their pain—and he cared.

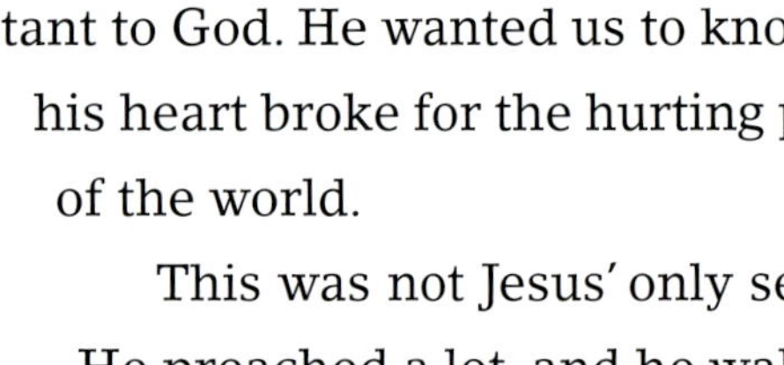

Jesus knew that one day you and I might wonder what is important to God. He wanted us to know that his heart broke for the hurting people of the world.

This was not Jesus' only sermon. He preached a lot, and he walked to and fro among the villages and towns of Judea. In every town he entered, he spoke about God's Kingdom to all who would listen.

He told them that God's Kingdom was a Kingdom of love and truth and joy and compassion. To join God's Kingdom, people had to repent and admit that they hadn't been living the way God wanted them to live.

It is hard to admit when you are wrong. We want to believe that we are always honest and good. But sometimes we are mean. The good news of the Kingdom is that meanness does not win. Our wrong choices and bad days do not have to be the end of our story. We can start over. This is true whether we are rich or poor. Anyone can start over and decide to follow Jesus.

Lots of people decided to take Jesus up on his offer to start again. Many of these people had hard lives. They were poor or sick or both. Jesus healed them of their physical diseases to show them that God wanted to heal the deepest parts of them. God wanted to heal their hearts.

This was the work that God sent Jesus to do: to heal all the things that were broken. He did his job well.

THE GOSPELS

A Strange Kingdom

The kingdom of God has come near.
Repent and believe the good news!
Mark 1:15

Four books in the Bible are known as the Gospels: Matthew, Mark, Luke, and John. All tell the story of Jesus. It was like the story was too good to just tell once—the Bible had to tell it four times! These stories have a lot in common.

There was one story Jesus told over and over: the story of the Kingdom.

Wherever Jesus and his disciples went, he told people, "Repent, for the Kingdom of God is here."

Have you ever heard something at school that made you wonder, *What does that mean?* The Kingdom of God is a little confusing and tricky to understand. Let's talk about kings and kingdoms.

The people of Israel had some good kings—but mostly bad kings. The bad kings did cruel things. They didn't take care of the people. They built fancy palaces and ate the most delicious food while the people of Israel went hungry and were left without a warm place to lay their heads. With the bad kings in charge, the poor suffered.

The people began to hope God would be their King. The Holy Spirit inspired prophets like Isaiah to describe what it would be like when God's Kingdom came. They reminded people that it was God, after all, who rescued them from slavery. God was a better King than any human.

Many Israelites thought that when God became King, everything would suddenly be better. God would kick out all the mean people and give rewards to the good people. Who doesn't love rewards?

Have you ever waited for a parent to pick you up from school when you were hurt or sick? Once they showed up, everything was okay. That's what it was like for the Israelites to dream about God's Kingdom. When God became King, there would be justice for everyone. There would be no more war or sickness or hunger.

Jesus said, "The Kingdom of God is here through me!"

"When I heal the sick, that is God's healing power come close."

"When I give food to the hungry, that is God's ability to provide come close."

"When I forgive sins, that is God's power to make new come close."

"When I raise the dead, that is God's power over life and death come close."

"When I tell stories about forgiveness, mercy, and love, that is God's picture of the good life come close."

God's rule had finally arrived. Jesus stepped into the starring role in a story that began before the world was created.

But it became clear that God's Kingdom was a strange Kingdom.

In the stories of David and the kings of Israel, the king's army fought battles against their enemies. David defeated Goliath.

The judges overcame stronger and better-trained armies. When we imagine heroes today, we think of swords and punches. Aren't heroes supposed to fight?

Instead of fighting, Jesus healed. He loved. He told even the worst bad guys and bad girls that God loved them and forgave them. What kind of hero forgives the villain?

Jesus knew that our biggest enemies were not other people, but sin, spiritual powers, and death. These were the enemies Jesus came to fight. Not with swords and shields but by sacrificing himself on the Cross.

Through his death and resurrection, Jesus won the greatest victory ever. He defeated the scariest enemy: death itself. The Kingdom that Jesus came to establish does not end. It has no borders. Being part of the Kingdom means living with God. But we are getting ahead of ourselves by telling this part of the story. More on this soon.

Every one of Jesus' miracles was a picture of what his Kingdom is like. Jesus healed because one day when he comes back, he will end sickness. Jesus gave food to the hungry because in God's Kingdom, there will be enough for everyone. Jesus forgave people who did bad things because forgiveness is a way of life in God's Kingdom. Jesus showed compassion because in God's Kingdom, everyone receives mercy. Jesus was God's Kingdom in person.

How did people join this Kingdom? Jesus said you must repent to be part of his Kingdom. Do you remember the definition of *repent*? It means to turn away from a life without God and turn toward a life with God. Since anyone can turn away from sin, anyone can be a part of God's Kingdom. People from every nation in the world have taken him up on the offer. It is a wonderful offer. It is good news.

Parents tell their kids the same things over and over. They remind their kids to brush their teeth or clean their rooms. They say, "Be kind to your little brother" or "Share your toys with your sister" or "Take turns."

Jesus said the same thing over and over to all who would listen: "Repent, for the strange and beautiful Kingdom of God is here!"

JOHN 10:1-18

Jesus, the Good Shepherd

I have other sheep that are not of this sheep pen.
I must bring them also. They too will listen to my voice,
and there shall be one flock and one shepherd.
John 10:16

I have a lot of different titles that tell people about me. My kids call me dad. *Dad* means love and protection. I am the one they turn to when they are hurt or sad. My wife calls me husband. My students call me professor. All these titles talk about parts of me. Jesus had lots of titles that help us know him better. He was a king because God chose him to rule. He was a prophet because he pointed the people back to God and to justice. One title that Jesus gave himself was the Good Shepherd.

Sheep are not very good at looking after themselves. They need someone to show them where to find food. They need someone to

protect them from danger. They get lost very easily. Sheep aren't the smartest animals in the world.

Jesus said, "I am the Good Shepherd" because God sent him to take care of his people the way a shepherd takes care of his sheep. He came to earth so his people could have a life that overflows with love and care.

We might be able to find food in the refrigerator and water from the faucet, but we still need someone to take care of us.

Not all of Israel's leaders were good shepherds like Jesus. Many of them did not care for Israel. Instead of helping the people, they took advantage of them. Jesus described these leaders as thieves and robbers. They didn't love God's sheep well.

Bad shepherds were not limited to Israel. The world had bad shepherds all over—and it still does. Many leaders did not care enough about those who were hurting, sick, or hungry. As Jesus said, they cared only about themselves.

Jesus also said, "My sheep know something is wrong when a thief or a robber calls them. They only listen to my voice."

Jesus' followers knew that he was different. They could hear the love and concern in his voice. They followed him.

Have you ever been lost and scared, and all of a sudden you heard your parents calling your name? You heard the love in their voices and knew you were safe. That's what it was like to see Jesus in Israel. His teachings and his miracles and healings made the people feel safe and loved. His life brought people back to God.

But how can we know that Jesus really is the Good Shepherd? So many other people have claimed to be loving leaders, but then they hurt their people. Jesus said, "You can know that I am the Good Shepherd because I lay down my life for the sheep." Jesus loved his sheep enough to die for them—for us.

When Jesus called himself the Good Shepherd, he was speaking to the lost sheep of Israel. But he also had other followers who didn't know him yet.

He said, "I have sheep in other places. I must go get them as well." The other sheep are all the different peoples of the world. These sheep are Asians and Africans, Europeans, North and South Americans. They are Kenyans, Nigerians, Ugandans, Germans, Italians, Guatemalans, Puerto Ricans, Thai, Chinese, Indians, and Japanese. The sheep are everywhere. They are the people of the world whom Jesus finds and brings home.

When Jesus mentioned these other sheep, he was talking about God's promise to bring people from every nation into his Kingdom. God wants people of all shapes, sizes, colors, and abilities in his family.

Then Jesus said, "There will be one flock and one shepherd." Although we are all different, we are united by the love of our Good Shepherd: the one who died for us so we could be part of his flock.

MARK 15:21-32

The Cross That Brings the Nations

And I, when I am lifted up from the earth,
will draw all people to myself.
John 12:32

For Simon, it was a normal day in Jerusalem. He had come with his family from Cyrene in North Africa to worship God during the season of Passover. Do you remember the story of Passover from earlier in this book? This holiday celebrates God's great rescue of his people from slavery in Egypt. Simon sat around a table with his fellow Jews and remembered God's miracle. He wondered when God would do something like that again.

He had no idea that he was about to play a small role in God's greatest act of deliverance ever: the salvation that would come from the death and resurrection of Jesus.

Simon was making his way back to the city from the countryside when he saw a commotion. A crowd of people, including several soldiers, were following a man down the road as he carried a heavy wooden cross. Simon stopped a member of the crowd and asked, "Who is this? What is going on?"

The man answered impatiently, "This is Jesus of Nazareth—the one who performed all the miracles and claimed to be the Messiah.

He was sentenced to death by crucifixion by Pontius Pilate for claiming to be king of the Jews." (Calling yourself the king of the Jews was illegal because the Romans saw it as rebellion against their empire.)

Simon saw Jesus, tired and bloody, and something stirred in him. He felt sorry for this man. Then Simon made eye contact with a soldier, who yelled, "Hey, you. Come here!"

Simon knew better than to upset a Roman official, so he went quickly.

The soldier said, "He is too weak to carry this cross. Help him!"

Simon did as he was told. During Jesus' last hours on this earth, Simon walked beside him, helping carry his cross. As they walked, Simon thought, *There is something about this man. He is no common criminal.* His heart was moved by Jesus.

Simon walked with Jesus all the way up the hill, and then he slid back into the crowd, shaken by what he had experienced.

There is something odd about this story.

How do we know Simon's name today? Did he say, "My name is Simon!" when the soldier asked him to carry the cross? That is not very likely.

How do we know that his children were named Rufus and Alexander? Did Simon tell the soldier the names of his children? No.

We know his name because Simon became a Christian. Someone must have told him that the person he carried the cross for had defeated death and sin. After Jesus rose again, Simon believed this good news and told his sons about it too.

Simon, Alexander, and Rufus were an early Christian family. An African Jew carried the cross and joined God's new family after the Resurrection. God's plan of gathering a diverse family had never

stopped. God always wanted a beautifully diverse family gathered around the cross. Simon was just the beginning.

But why did Jesus have to die?

Jesus died to show us how far God's love reaches. He paid the penalty that we deserve and made it possible for us to turn toward him. We are all born running. We run away from God and truth and goodness. Sometimes we do good things and sometimes we are cruel, but without God's help, we always run from him.

Sometimes I catch my daughters or my sons sneaking candy or drawing on the wall. When I ask them if they did it, they become sad. They are sad because they know that they have done something wrong. Sometimes when they are sad, they hide.

All of us hide from our sins. But hiding does not fool anyone. When we come out of our rooms or wherever we're hiding, the problem will still be there. Running won't fix it.

The problem of sin was too big for humans to solve. We needed a God who loved us enough to save us from our sin. We needed someone to heal us.

Jesus died to heal us.

The Cross is Jesus taking the punishment for our sins and giving us the medicine for our healing. The Cross means that we do not have to hide anymore.

When my daughter drew on the wall, it left a mark that everyone could see. There was evidence of her mistake. But I washed it away. Now it's not there anymore. It's all gone.

On the Cross, Jesus takes away all the bad things that we've done. The Bible says that our sins were taken away, nailed to the Cross.

To be a Christian is to accept God's offer of healing that comes from the Cross. It is the best news.

MATTHEW 28:1-20

He Is Not Here; He Is Risen!

Do not be afraid, for I know that you are looking for Jesus, who was crucified. He is not here; he has risen, just as he said.
Matthew 28:5-6

When Jesus died on the Cross, it seemed like a defeat. But God is good at turning defeats into victories.

After Jesus died, most of his disciples gave up hope. They hid and wondered if they might be next. The women who followed Jesus didn't know what to do after he died. But one of them had an idea: the least they could do was honor his body.

Mary Magdalene and another woman named Mary said, "Let's go to the tomb and pour oil and spices on Jesus' body."

"How will we get to him with that huge stone in front of the tomb?" the second Mary wondered.

"We'll cross that bridge when we come to it," said Mary Magdalene. "Let's go!"

Early Sunday morning, the women made their way to the tomb. When they arrived, the ground beneath their feet started to shake. Something strange was happening. It was an earthquake!

The earthquake must have been very scary for these women. It would scare me!

Next, something even more terrifying took place. An angel came down from heaven. He was as bright as lightning, and the women's jaws dropped in unison. All the air fled their lungs in a whoosh.

The angel rolled away the stone in front of the tomb. That problem was solved with a flourish. The guards who were keeping watch over the tomb were so afraid they started trembling and fell to the ground like dead men.

The angel said to the women, "Do not be afraid. I know that you are looking for Jesus, who was crucified. He is not here. He is risen, just as he promised. Come see the place where his body lay. Then go tell his disciples." Jesus had told his disciples that he would rise from the dead, but they had not understood.

I have surprised my family with good news before. Sometimes I bring home dinner from their favorite fast-food restaurant. Sometimes we have movie nights even when there is school the next day. But I have never had news as good as the news these women shared. God gave them the best, biggest news in human history. Jesus had defeated death. There could not be a more important story. God trusted these women to tell the story so people would know forever that both men and women can share the good news. We are all God's missionaries.

On their way to tell the other disciples, the women met Jesus.

The words of the angel were true! He had indeed risen from the dead.

Now that not even death could hold Jesus, there was nothing for his people to fear. If the death of Jesus was the world's saddest day, his resurrection was the day filled with the most joy. And this joy is not just for you and me. It is for the whole world.

Jesus met up with the rest of his disciples in Galilee. Some were excited, and some were scared. It may seem weird to be afraid *after* Jesus defeated death, but such a big surprise was very hard to understand.

Jesus gave his disciples an important job before he went back to heaven. He said, "God has given me all authority on earth and in heaven. I am giving you a mission. Go and make disciples of all the different peoples of the world. Teach them all that I taught you." That includes everything Jesus said about love, obedience, justice, and compassion. "Baptize them in the name of the Father, the Son, and the Holy Spirit. No matter what happens, know that I am with you. Even to the very end of the age."

God's great story began with a heart open to the world. Now, after his Son's resurrection, that story continued. We are Christians today because somebody listened to Jesus and brought the good news of his love to us and our family. There are Christians on every continent. There are Christians of every color. God's plan is unfolding. His family is growing. His work continues through us.

ACTS 1:1-14; 2:1-41

Pentecost: The Spirit Is for Everyone

In the last days, God says, I will pour out my Spirit on all people. Your sons and daughters will prophesy, your young men will see visions, your old men will dream dreams.
Acts 2:17

After God raised Jesus from the dead, he appeared to many of his disciples.

Before he returned to rule beside his Father in heaven, Jesus gave them instructions: stay in Jerusalem and wait for the Holy Spirit to come to them.

Jesus told them, "You will tell people about who I am and the things that I did in Jerusalem, Samaria, and the whole world."

What a big mission! Who could do a job that big? The good news is that it would not be the disciples' mission alone. God would give them the Spirit to help them and strengthen them to do the work he told them to do.

Fifty days after the resurrection of Jesus, on a day known as Pentecost, all of Jesus' followers—the apostles, Jesus' mother, his brothers, and other women—gathered in prayer.

A noise came from heaven. It sounded like a windstorm. Jesus' followers saw what looked like tongues made of fire. These flames rested on all of them, the men and the women. The Spirit of God filled them all. The Spirit gave them the ability to speak in languages they did not know before.

At the time, there were Jews from all over the world in Jerusalem. They were amazed when they heard their own languages being spoken. "These are local Jews from Galilee," the visitors said. "How is it possible that they are using our languages to tell about the wonderful things God has done?"

How would it feel if you showed up at school one day with the ability to speak any language? People would be surprised and a little scared. You might be a little scared.

Some people wanted to know the meaning of what was happening. Other people made fun of Jesus' followers. It is easy to make fun of what we do not understand. It's important to pay attention to what God is doing around us even if it seems strange.

Why did God allow all the different people visiting Jerusalem to hear the good news in their own languages? God wanted to show everyone that no matter where they came from, they were welcome in his family. The many languages were a picture of a Kingdom made up of different people.

It was kind of like when you're trying to pick a movie and you watch the trailer. The trailer does not tell you everything. It's a preview of what to expect if you watch the whole movie.

The miracle of Pentecost didn't tell us everything about God's Kingdom, but it did show a preview of what God's family was going to be like: many different types of people who share the same faith.

Peter, one of the leaders of the early church, stood up at Pentecost to explain what was going on. "A long time ago, God gave a prophecy to a man named Joel. This prophecy showed that one day, God would give his Spirit to all people—the young and the old, the enslaved and the free, the men and the women. It would be a time of salvation and judgment. When that day came, everyone who called out for the Lord's help would be saved."

Becoming more confident, Peter told the story of Jesus. "Men of Israel, pay attention. Jesus of Nazareth was a man who had God's seal of approval. Jesus made God's approval clear by the wonders and signs he did. But he was put to death on a cross. Even his death was a part of God's plan. Death was not powerful enough to hold him. God raised Jesus from the dead. We, his disciples, are all witnesses of this. This Jesus who was crucified—God has made him Lord and Savior."

These words made the people wonder what they had to do for Jesus to save them. Peter told them, "Repent and be baptized in Jesus' name to have your sins forgiven. You will receive the Holy Spirit. This gift is for you and your children and for everyone God calls into his family."

Peter's words were a miracle. Jesus offered forgiveness to everyone, even the people who handed him over to the Romans to be crucified. He died and rose again to bring us back to God. Jesus is God's love reaching out to grab us by the arm and wrap us in a big hug. There is nothing you can do that's so bad God cannot forgive you. His love is huge.

God invited people who spoke all the different languages of the world into his family. Over three thousand people from all over the earth heard Peter's message on Pentecost and believed in Jesus. God's big diverse family was continuing to grow.

ACTS 8:1-40

The Ethiopian Eunuch: The Gospel Goes Out to the World

"Do you understand what you are reading?" Philip asked. "How can I," he said, "unless someone explains it to me?" So he invited Philip to come up and sit with him.
Acts 8:30-31

The church that started at Pentecost continued to grow. It grew even though some people wanted to stop the church from spreading. Because things were dangerous in Jerusalem, many Christians had to leave and go somewhere else. As they went to different places, they told the story of Jesus.

One person who left Jerusalem was named Philip. He went to Samaria and told the people there that Jesus was the long-expected King. God gave Philip the power to heal many sick people and perform miracles. The city rejoiced that he was there. The people of Samaria—known as Samaritans—were a different ethnic group than the Jews. Jews and Samaritans did not usually get along, but the gospel can turn enemies into friends.

The gospel coming to the Samaritans was part of God's plan. Jesus told his disciples that they would be his witnesses in Jerusalem, Samaria, and to the ends of the earth. God used Philip and others like him to make his plans succeed.

The Samaritans were happy because Philip served people like Jesus did. The church, acting like Jesus, is a source of joy. Living like Jesus at school and home makes you a source of joy even if you don't give sight to the blind.

Just when things seemed to be going well in Samaria, an angel of the Lord told Philip, "Travel south to a road that goes from Jerusalem to Gaza." That must have seemed like a strange command, but Philip obeyed.

On his way to Gaza, Philip met an Ethiopian eunuch. He was in charge of the money for the queen of Ethiopia. Eunuchs were boys taken from their families to serve the royal family. They had a surgery when they were young that kept them from ever becoming fathers, and they were not given a choice. Many times they were mistreated, and they often felt ashamed. This eunuch had an important job in Ethiopia, but he also felt alone.

The Ethiopian was on his way home from Jerusalem, where he had gone to worship God. The Holy Spirit told Philip to go up to the eunuch's chariot. When Philip ran up beside the chariot, he heard the man reading the book of Isaiah out loud.

Philip asked him, "Do you understand what you are reading?"

The Ethiopian eunuch answered, "How can I, unless someone explains it to me?"

This was the passage he was reading:

> He was led like a lamb to the slaughter, and he was silent like a lamb being shaved. He did not open his mouth. In his humiliation, he did not receive justice.

Why did the Ethiopian read this passage? Maybe because the story of someone denied justice was similar to his own. Maybe the Ethiopian felt like people had forced him to be quiet too.

"Who is the prophet Isaiah is talking about—himself or someone else?" the Ethiopian asked.

Philip was happy to answer this question. "Isaiah shared this prophecy about an innocent person who would be treated unfairly and killed. This person's suffering would bring healing to the nations," Philip explained. "Jesus is this person! He is the innocent one who suffered for the healing of the world—not just for Israel. This healing and forgiveness is available to people from every country. All you have to do is put your faith in Jesus and be baptized."

"There is some water over there!" the Ethiopian said. "What's stopping me from getting baptized?"

Philip baptized him, and then the Spirit told him to travel somewhere else. The Ethiopian, full of joy, went back home.

The early years of the church were full of excitement and

miracles. There were too many stories to tell. It was like trying to tell someone everything you did during the summer. You have to leave out a lot and only include the best parts.

Luke, who wrote the story of the early church in the book of Acts, had to make choices. He could only include the best parts that God wanted everyone to know about. Of all the stories he could have written down, the story of the Ethiopian eunuch was one of the most important.

Why? The prophet Isaiah might help. He wrote about non-Israelites and eunuchs who might think God doesn't care about them. Isaiah told them that God wants them in his family.

God inspired Luke to tell this story so all people—whether they're African like the Ethiopian or from Korea or Pakistan or Italy or Colombia or the United States—would know God wants them. If you have a disability or an injury, God wants you, too. He wants us all.

ACTS 9–28

Paul, Apostle to the Nations

This man is my chosen instrument to proclaim my name to the Gentiles and their kings and to the people of Israel.
Acts 9:15

When his story began, the person we know as Paul the apostle was not happy that people were spreading the word about Jesus. He did not believe that Jesus was the promised King of Israel. He thought, *A crucified king is impossible. God is calling me to put a stop to this Christian movement! I will lock them in jail if I have to.* He even approved of killing Christians.

It did not matter if you were a girl or a boy. If you followed Jesus, Paul wanted to stop you.

On his way to Damascus to arrest more Christians, Paul's life changed forever. As he walked down the road, a flash of light from heaven appeared around him. He fell to the ground.

Then he heard a voice: "Paul, Paul, why are you trying to hurt me?"

Paul answered him, "Who are you, Lord?"

"I am Jesus, the one you are hurting."

Paul was confused. When had he hurt Jesus? He didn't realize that if you attack Jesus' people, you are attacking him. We are united with Jesus. He cares about what happens to us.

Jesus said, "Stand up and go into the city. Then I will tell you what comes next."

When Paul got up from the ground, he was blind. But the men traveling with him helped him get to Damascus.

Once Paul arrived in the city, Jesus appeared to Ananias, a Christian man who lived there. Jesus told him, "Go to Judas's house on Straight Street. Ask for a guy named Paul from Tarsus. He is praying, and he saw a vision that you would come and give him back his sight."

Ananias answered, "I've heard of Paul. He hurt a lot of Christians in Jerusalem. He has come here to cause more trouble."

"Do as I said," Jesus replied. "I have chosen Paul to spread my message to all the different ethnic groups and their kings, as well as to the people of Israel. Things will be hard for him, but he will do all this for me."

Ananias got up quickly and did what Jesus told him to do. He told Paul, "Jesus sent me so you could be healed and filled with the Holy Spirit." Paul regained his sight and got baptized.

After his baptism, Paul began to do the work that God gave him. He traveled around the whole Roman Empire starting churches made up of all different types of people. Some were

rich and some were poor. Some were Jewish and some were not. Despite their differences, they shared the same faith in Jesus.

Paul preached the same message everywhere. He said, "Jesus is God's Son and Israel's long-hoped-for King. All God's plans and promises come together in Jesus." He told people that God would save them if they declared that Jesus was Lord and believed that God raised him from the dead.

"Jesus is a strange kind of King. He is a King who loves his people and died for them. Jesus was a crucified King who rose again."

This message got Paul in trouble. People ran him out of many towns. He was hit with rocks and beaten and thrown in jail. But it was worth it for Paul because he knew that the job of spreading God's message to the different peoples of the world was the most important thing he could do. The news was too good to keep to himself.

Life in the churches that Paul started was not always easy. Just like families who love one another still fight, so do churches. They made mistakes. They sin. Paul wrote letters to the early churches. He helped them remember what God did for them and how they should live.

Sometimes Paul helped settle fights between Jews and non-Jews. Paul fought to keep them together in the church. He wanted Jews and non-Jews together because he knew that's what God wanted. Different types of people worshiping God together painted a picture of what God's Kingdom looked like. Paul fought as hard as he could to keep all the different parts of God's family together. He knew we needed each other.

Having faith in Jesus is enough to be made right with God. No other rules are needed!

THE BOOK OF GALATIANS

Paul's Letter to the Galatians

All of you who were baptized into Christ have clothed yourselves with Christ. There is neither Jew nor Gentile, neither slave nor free, nor is there male and female, for you are all one in Christ Jesus. If you belong to Christ, then you are Abraham's seed, and heirs according to the promise.
Galatians 3:27-29

All families have disagreements. Some are small. Some are big. Paul started a church in a place called Galatia. At first, everything was great.

After Paul left Galatia, though, some other Christians came in with new rules. As you can imagine, Paul was not happy that people tried to change things so soon after he started this church!

These other Christians told the Galatians that God wanted more from them than just faith. They said God wanted the Galatians to keep the Old Testament laws, including those that told the people what food they could eat.

Paul wrote to the Galatians, "Having faith in Jesus is enough to be made right with God. No other rules are needed!"

This may seem like a strange thing for a kid to care about. It is not very likely that your pastor or parents are telling you that you must follow certain Old Testament laws to be a Christian.

But Paul thought it was very important to write about this. Why?

Paul remembered what God's big story was all about. This big story was God's plan to create one family made up of people from all over the world. He knew that the church was supposed to be "Here comes everybody."

So how are we made right with God? What makes us members of his family?

When people throw birthday parties, they often send out invitations. The invitations are your ticket to the fun. If Latasha Johnson hosts a birthday party and you show up with an invitation from Jason Kim, they might not let you in.

What do you need to have on your invitation to become part of God's family? How do you get into the party?

Paul told the Galatians, "Meeting the requirements of the law does not make us right with God. We are made right with God by believing in what the Messiah—Jesus—did for us." Paul believed that the law was a good thing—after all, God provided it to show his people how to live. But following the law was not a requirement to be in God's family. There are no requirements other than trusting in Jesus.

Paul knew that this was true whether you were Jewish or non-Jewish, male or female, enslaved or free. None of those things get you special perks from God. All that matters to him is that we repent and believe.

Why do we have to trust Jesus? Why not follow the whole law instead?

The law has two parts: the blessings if you obey and the punishments if you disobey.

HAPPY BIRTHDAY

If you've gotten this far in the book, you probably remember that Israel had a hard time following the law. Why couldn't they do it? That's a good question! The Israelites struggled to keep the law because they were human beings. All human beings do bad things because sin is in us and in the world.

There has only ever been one person who never sinned. Only one person who deserved all of God's blessings. That person was Jesus. He obeyed the law perfectly, and he took the punishment due for those who disobeyed the law. The worst of these punishments was death. When Jesus died on the Cross, he paid the full price for sin. Once he was raised from the dead, the punishment for sin had no more power over those who put their faith in him.

Jesus accepted the consequences we deserve and gave us the blessings that *he* deserved. What a wonderful exchange!

Paul said, "Christians are led by God's Spirit. Living by the Spirit produces fruit. The fruit of the Spirit is love, joy, peace, patience, kindness, goodness, faithfulness, gentleness, and self-control. There are no laws against doing the things the Spirit wants us to do."

In this letter, Paul wrote about one more thing God gave his people: the church. Paul told the Galatians that they did not have to go through life alone. They could help each other out with their problems. And that's still true today.

Christians are brothers and sisters. What makes the church a family isn't that we all look alike. We don't. What makes the church a family is that we believe in the same God. Paul knew that the church and the Spirit could help Christians live lives that bring God glory.

THE BOOK OF JAMES

James's Letter

Look! The wages you failed to pay the workers who mowed your fields are crying out against you. The cries of the harvesters have reached the ears of the Lord Almighty.
James 5:4

James was Jesus' brother. Lots of us have family members who do cool things. My older sister is a medical doctor. My younger sister is a chef. My younger brother played professional sports. But none of my siblings are God.

James grew up with Jesus, but he also became a person who worshiped Jesus. Jesus *must* have been God to get his family to join his church. I know that I wouldn't join a church dedicated to my sister!

James wrote letters to mostly Jewish Christian churches. He gave them advice about how to live for God. James and Paul spoke to different types of churches. God used them both.

People in James's churches had bad things happen to them. James gave them some advice that may seem odd: "Have joy when life gets hard. Hard times make your faith strong. Strong faith helps you become a better Christian."

James reminded them, "If you have money and power, that shouldn't make you proud. It does not matter if you have a nice house or fancy clothes or expensive shoes because that is not what God cares about. It will all go away one day."

Poor Christians could take comfort in James's words: "Remember that God your Father made everything and has everything." James believed that faith in Jesus lifted up the poor and humbled the rich so that they could meet in the same place as family. Jesus brings unity.

James also taught the churches about the power of words. He told them, "Be careful about what you say to each other because words matter. They can bring life or destruction. Your words can be a blessing or a curse." We can hurt people with the things we say and make them feel like God doesn't love them. But the opposite is true too!

James warned the rich, "Cry and moan because you will be punished. Your money will rot and your clothes will be ruined." That sounds harsh. Why did James say this? Did James hate people with money? No. He didn't like the way that wealthy people treated their workers. "The fact that you don't pay your workers is evidence against you. God hears the cries of the workers you refuse to pay."

James knew that it matters how we treat each other. The words we say matter. The way we treat the poor and the worker matters. James was like his brother Jesus in this way. He cared about fair treatment. He cared about justice.

THE BOOK OF REVELATION

How the Story Ends

After this I looked, and there before me was a great multitude that no one could count, from every nation, tribe, people and language, standing before the throne and before the Lamb. They were wearing white robes and were holding palm branches in their hands. And they cried out in a loud voice: "Salvation belongs to our God, who sits on the throne, and to the Lamb."

Revelation 7:9-10

The beginning of a story is important, and so is the ending. We are at the end of our story now. The last book of the Bible is called Revelation. The apostle John wrote it to help Christians learn how to live now by understanding God's future plan for the world. John was one of the apostles who followed Jesus from the beginning. By the time he wrote this story, most of the other apostles had died. The Romans had sent John to an island called Patmos because they did not want him to spread the story of Jesus. But a little thing like exile to an island couldn't stop the gospel.

Revelation tells stories of visions that God showed John. There are many things I would love to see. I would love to see my favorite professional sports team play in the championship game. John got to witness something even better. He got to see what things will be like in the future when God makes all things new.

What was in this vision of the future? What did John see? He witnessed a great crowd of people from all the nations, tribes, peoples, and languages of the world. They were standing in front of the Lamb's throne. (John calls Jesus the Lamb because he was sacrificed for us like lambs were sacrificed in the Old Testament.) This crowd was worshiping God, singing, "Salvation belongs to God who sits on the throne and to the Lamb."

When John glimpsed the very end of the story, people from every nation on the globe were there. He saw a worldwide party. The party was very diverse, and every language was ringing out. Why were all these people united? Because they loved the same God. God's plan for a big diverse family will come true one day, and it will be just like this.

John saw another vision. This vision showed him a beautiful new world. The world we live in now is full of sin, sadness, and death. When Jesus comes back, he will end sin and death forever. His world will be full of life and love.

The new world will have a holy city: the New Jerusalem. God and his family will live there together forever. All the sad things will be gone, and God will wipe away all of our tears.

In this vision, John saw a river. It flowed out from God's throne. On both sides of the river was the tree of life. John said that in the new world, it will provide healing for the nations.

John knew that life was not easy. He knew that sometimes life would make us cry. Our tears are not the end of the story. The fighting and meanness are not the end of the story. The story does not end with God's people divided. The story ends with people from all the nations of the world healed by the tree of life. The tree will be open to everyone when God's Kingdom arrives on earth. Jesus hasn't returned yet, but his Kingdom is already open because he made a way for us by dying on the Cross and rising again.

God is at work creating this beautifully diverse family, just as he said he would. One day Jesus will come back, establish his Kingdom, and gather this family together. Until he does, we'll worship him. We'll live for him. We'll tell the world the greatest story ever until the King comes again in his glory.

Acknowledgments

I would like to thank the team at Tyndale for their diligence in putting this all together, especially Linda Howard, who first approached me with the idea of doing a children's Bible.

About the Author

Rev. Esau McCaulley, PhD, is associate professor of New Testament and the Jonathan Blanchard Chair of New Testament and Public Theology at Wheaton College in Wheaton, Illinois. Rev. McCaulley also serves as the rector (senior pastor) of All Saints Anglican Church in Naperville, Illinois. He is the author of the children's books *Andy Johnson and the March for Justice* and *Josey Johnson's Hair and the Holy Spirit*. For adults he has written many other works including *How Far to the Promised Land: One Black Family's Story of Hope and Survival in the American South* and *Reading While Black: African American Biblical Interpretation as an Exercise in Hope*. Dr. McCaulley is also a contributing opinion writer for the *New York Times*. His writings have appeared in *The Atlantic*, the *Washington Post*, and *Christianity Today*. He is a senior editor for Holy Post Media and hosts his own podcast there, creatively titled *The Esau McCaulley Podcast*. He is married to Mandy, a pediatrician and Navy reservist. Together, they have four wonderful children.

About the Illustrator

Rogério Coelho lives in Curitiba, a city in the south of Brazil. He has worked as a professional illustrator for twenty-five years, illustrating more than one hundred books for Brazilian publishers, and has twice received the Jabuti Award (2012 and 2016), Brazil's most important literary award. In 2015, Rogério began illustrating for publishers in England (*Storytime Magazine*, a magazine aimed at children) and in the United States. His wordless picture book *Boat of Dreams* received starred reviews from *School Library Journal* and *Booklist*, was named a Best Book for Kids by the New York Public Library in 2017, and received the Independent Publisher Book Awards' gold medal for children's picture books. Rogério also illustrated *You Be You* (written by Richard Brehm), which received the same gold medal for children's picture books in 2021.